T0315823

The Early Modern Englishwoman:
A Facsimile Library of Essential Works

Series II

Printed Writings, 1641–1700: Part 3

Volume 10

Fiction of Unknown or Questionable
Attribution, 2

Peppa *and* Alcander and Philocrates

The Early Modern Englishwoman:
A Facsimile Library of Essential Works

Series II

Printed Writings, 1641–1700: Part 3

Volume 10

Fiction of Unknown or Questionable
Attribution, 2

Peppa *and* Alcander and Philocrates

Selected and Introduced by
Erin Henriksen and Desma Polydorou

General Editors
Betty S. Travitsky and Anne Lake Prescott

ASHGATE

Published by
Ashgate Publishing Limited
Wey Court East
Union Road
Farnham
Surrey, GU9 7PT
England

Ashgate Publishing Company
110 Cherry Street
Suite 3-1
Burlington
VT 05401-3818
USA

Ashgate website: http://www.ashgate.com

British Library Cataloguing in Publication Data
Fiction of unknown or questionable attribution
2. – (The early modern Englishwoman : a facsimile library
of essential works. Series II Printed writings, 1641–1700 ;
pt. 3, v. 10)
1.French fiction – 17th century – Translations into English
2.Women and literature – Great Britain – History – 17th
century 3.English fiction – Early modern, 1500–1700
4.English fiction – Women authors
I.Henriksen, Erin II.Polydorou, Desma III.Peppa IV.Alcander
and Philocrates
843.4'0809287 [F]

Library of Congress Cataloging-in-Publication Data
The early modern Englishwoman: a facsimile library of essential works. Printed writings, 1641–1700 / general editors, Betty S. Travitsky and Anne Lake Prescott.

See page vi for complete CIP Block

The image reproduced on the title page and on the case is from the frontispiece portrait in *Poems. By the Most Deservedly Admired Mrs. Katherine Philips* (1667). Reproduced by permission of the Folger Shakespeare Library, Washington, DC.

ISBN 978-0-7546-0987-2   Transferred to Digital Printing in 2011

MIX
Paper from
responsible sources
FSC® C004959
www.fsc.org

Printed and bound in Great Britain
by Printondemand-worldwide.com

CONTENTS

Library of Congress Cataloging-in-Publication Data

Fiction of unknown or questionable attribution / selected and introduced by Erin Henriksen
and Desma Polydorou

    p cm. – (The early modern Englishwoman. Printed Writings, 1641–1700, Series 2, Part
3 ; 9-10)

    Includes bibliographical references.

    Contents 1 Diotrephe, or, An historie of valentines / written in French by John Peter
Camus ; [translated by S du Verger]. The amorous abbess, or, Love in a nunnery /
[written by Sébastien Brémond] ; translated from the French by a Woman of quality – 2.
Peppa, or, The reward of constant love . a novel : done out of French . with several songs
set to musick, for two voices / by a Young-gentlewoman [A.C.] Alcander and Philocrates,
or, The pleasures and disquietudes of marriage / written by a Young lady.

    ISBN 0-7546-0219-2 (v 1 · alk. paper) – ISBN 0–7546–0987–1 (v. 2 : alk. paper)

    1 English fiction–Early modern, 1500–1700. 2 French fiction–Translations into
English 3. Women translators–Great Britain 4. English fiction–Women authors 5.
Anonymous writings, English. I. Henriksen, Erin II Polydourou, Desma. III. Du Verger,
S. IV. Woman of quality V Camus, Jean-Pierre, 1584–1652 Diotrephe English. VI.
Brémond, Sébastien, b 1645 Cercle. English. Selections VII A C Peppa English VIII
Young lady. Alcander and Philcrates, or, The pleasures and disquietudes of marriage. IX.
Title: Diotrephe, or, An historie of valentines X. Title· Historie of valentines. XI. Title·
Amorous abbess, or, Love in a nunnery XII Title. Reward of constant love. XIII. Title·
Peppa, or, The reward of constant love XIV Title Alcander and Philocrates, or, The
pleasures and disquietudes of marriage. XV Title. Pleasures and disquietudes of marriage.
– Series.

PR1295.F53 2004
823' 408–dc22

                                        2004048255

PREFACE
BY THE GENERAL EDITORS

Until very recently, scholars of the early modern period have assumed that there were no Judith Shakespeares in early modern England. Much of the energy of the current generation of scholars has been devoted to constructing a history of early modern England that takes into account what women actually wrote, what women actually read, and what women actually did. In so doing, contemporary scholars have revised the traditional representation of early modern women as constructed both in their own time and in ours. The study of early modern women has thus become one of the most important – indeed perhaps the most important – means for the rewriting of early modern history.

The Early Modern Englishwoman: A Facsimile Library of Essential Works is one of the developments of this energetic reappraisal of the period. As the names on our advisory board and our list of editors testify, it has been the beneficiary of scholarship in the field, and we hope it will also be an essential part of that scholarship's continuing momentum.

The Early Modern Englishwoman is designed to make available a comprehensive and focused collection of writings in English from 1500 to 1750, both by women and for and about them. The three series of *Printed Writings* (1500–1640, 1641–1700, and 1701–1750) provide a comprehensive if not entirely complete collection of the separately published writings by women. In reprinting these writings we intend to remedy one of the major obstacles to the advancement of feminist criticism of the early modern period, namely the limited availability of the very texts upon which the field is based. The volumes in the facsimile library reproduce carefully chosen copies of these texts, incorporating significant variants (usually in appendices). Each text is preceded by a short introduction providing an overview of the life and work of a writer along with a survey of important scholarship. These works, we strongly believe, deserve a large readership – of historians, literary critics, feminist critics, and non-specialist readers.

The Early Modern Englishwoman also includes separate facsimile series of *Essential Works for the Study of Early Modern Women* and of *Manuscript Writings*. These facsimile series are complemented by *The Early Modern Englishwoman 1500–1750: Contemporary Editions*. Also under our general editorship, this series includes both old-spelling and modernized editions of works by and about women and gender in early modern England.

New York City
2005

INTRODUCTORY NOTE

Four seventeenth-century novels that we have identified in the course of our ongoing research as 'fiction of unknown or uncertain female authorship, 1641–1700' are contained in these two volumes. Three of these novels are translations for which there is some evidence, whether internal or external, of female translators. In the course of preparing these volumes we uncovered additional works that may belong to the same categories of 'fiction of unknown or uncertain female authorship', suggesting the possibility of future additions to the present volumes. Because details of our effort to identify all published fiction written or translated by unnamed or unknown English women from 1641–1700 may prove helpful to those who may wish to attempt further recoveries, we begin with a sketch of our search.

We consulted ESTC online, Wing's *Short Title Catalogue* and the standard reference works on early modern women writers – including Bell, Parfitt and Shepherd's *A Biographical Dictionary of English Women Writers, 1580–1720*; Blain, Clements and Grundy's *The Feminist Companion to Literature in English*; Esdaile's *A List of English Tales and Prose Romances Printed Before 1740*; Mish's *English Prose Fiction, 1600–1700: a Chronological Checklist*; and Trill, Chedgzoy and Osborne's *Lay By Your Needles Ladies, Take the Pen*. We also consulted sources on anonymous and pseudonymous works, online catalogues (including the Folger Library and British Library catalogues), and the subject index of *Early English Books*, looking for works unsigned but perhaps by female authors or translators. This research generated a list of about two dozen works that required further inspection.

We eliminated several promising titles included in the standard catalogues and inventories after further examination. These include Sarah Davy's *Heaven Realiz'd, or The Holy Pleasure* (1670), which is an autobiographical religious narrative; Elizabeth Eyre's *A Letter from a Person of Quality* (1689), a text concerning official Anglican support of political obedience; *Maria to Henric, and Henric to Maria* (1691) and *Triumphs of Female Wit* (1683), both signed 'Young lady' but both written in verse; and *The Unnatural Mother* (1698), also signed 'Young lady', which is a drama. (Facsimiles of these texts have been included in other volumes in 'Printed Writings, 1641–1700'.)

We of course attempted to determine whether claims of female authorship or translation could be substantiated, and we excluded some other works when this attribution seemed merely to be a marketing ploy or could not be corroborated by any internal or external evidence. The many publications associated with Mary Carleton (Series II.3 of the facsimile library), a number of which are libels, illustrate the use of a woman's name to generate interest in a publication.

We also investigated and then eliminated from our list works of fiction that are unsigned or ascribed only to a set of initials, such as *The Amours of Bonne Sforza, Queen of Polonia* (1684). Its dedication is signed only 'P. B.', and there is no evidence to suggest that these initials represent a female author. Other works, attributed only to a 'Person of Quality', could potentially be the work of female authors, but no evidence has yet been found to validate this attribution for works such as *The Secret History of the Most Renowned Queen Elizabeth and the E. of Essex* (1680) and *The Pastime Royal* (1682).

We excluded works of fiction written by women in languages other than English or translated by English women from English into other languages. These include Marianna Alcoforado's *Five Love-letters from a Nun to a Cavalier* (1678) and *Seven Portuguese Letters* (1681); several works by Marie Catherine Hortense Desjardins, Madame de Villedieu; *The Count of Amboise* (1689) ('Written Originally In French by Madam ***' [Catherine Bernard]); and Maria Mancini's *The Apology, or, The genuine memoires of Madam Maria Manchini* (1679).

The chronological limits of the sub-series ('Printed Writings, 1641–1700') exclude works published after 1700. For some works, however, the dates of composition and publication are not clear. For instance, Mary Davys states in the preface to her collected works (*The Works of Mrs. Mary Davys* [1725]) that she wrote the novel *The Lady's Tale* in 1700, but an edition printed in that year has not been found, and the novel, therefore, has been excluded.

We discovered that most fiction written by English women from 1641 to 1700 was attributed to individual named authors (and therefore included in this facsimile series in the individual author volumes). Several novels associated with Mary Delarivier Manley are of disputed attribution, including *The Unhappy Lovers, Or, The Timorous Fair One* (1694) and *Vertue Rewarded, Or, The Irish Princess* (1693), as is some fiction associated with lesser-known figures, such as Mary Carleton and Catherine Cockburn Trotter.

Diotrephe, or an historie of Valentines (1641)

The only evidence for authorship of the English translation of *Diotrephe* is the signature of the dedicatory letter, 'S. du Verger'. Jane Collins suggests that the 'Susan du Vergeer' who translated *Admirable Events*, another novel by the author of *Diotrephe*, is identical to the 'S. du Verger' who translated *Diotrephe*, and that she may have written the English *Du Vergers Humble Reflections* (1657).

Diotrephe, set in the French city of Brianche, describes the practice of 'valentines', in which the names of all the women of the city are placed into a lottery and drawn by the men. Regardless of their marriages to others, the women and the men who draw their names become one another's valentines for one year. *Diotrephe* tells the story of two such couples: Theophane draws Nemese as his valentine after three years of marriage to Persidious. Theophane's friend Diotrephe, who is in love with Nemese, draws Persidious. Diotrephe's family is noble but impoverished, and he is befriended and funded by Calicrate, an Italian banker who also falls in love with and pursues Nemese. Diotrephe writes poetry to Nemese throughout the novel. (Both the French and English translations are included.)

The romantic confusion and betrayal that ensue from the assignment of valentines end in a duel between Theophane and Diotrephe in which Theophane dies and Diotrephe is maimed. The women both marry others and abjure the practice of valentines. The last ten pages of the novel are devoted to denouncing the immorality of the custom of valentines and emphasizing the sinfulness of following traditions rather than the word of God: 'the Law of God forbids adultery, yea or to covet your neighbours wife, and this tradition [that is, valentines], if it adulterise not, yet at least it alters just and lawfull affections' (182–83).

The original French novel, *Diotrephe: Histoire Valentine*, is by Jean-Pierre Camus (Lyon 1626). Camus, Bishop of Belley (1584–1652), wrote many religious works and several moralizing novels. Several were translated into English and printed in France and England: *Petronille* (Paris 1630), *A draught of eternitie* and *A spirituall combat* (both Douai 1632), *Elise* (London 1655), *Nature's paradox* (London 1652), *The spirituall director disinterested* (Paris 1633), and *A true tragical history of two illustrious Italian families* (London 1677).

The title *Diotrephe* may refer to Diotrephes ('Diotrephe' in French) in 3 John 9–10, who slanders the 'brethren' and casts them out of the church. In the Geneva Bible's dedication to Queen Elizabeth, Diotrephes is mentioned as an example of the ambitious prelate. The name also appears in several English works of the period, including William Prynne's *Diotrephes Catechised*, Laurence Womock's *The Result of False Principles*, and John Udall's *The State of the Church of Englande, Laide Open in a conference betweene Diotrephes a bishop, Tertullus a papist, Demetrius an usurer, Pandocheus an in-keeper, and Paule a preacher of the word of God*. The *Oxford English Dictionary* lists several other seventeenth-century instances.

Diotrephe was printed by Thomas Harper in 1641. Harper, a London printer from 1614 to 1656, was associated with many Catholic and Royalist publications. He was, says Plomer, occasionally in trouble for printing anti-Parliament works.

The copy of *Diotrephe* below is reproduced by permission of the Folger Shakespeare Library, with the exception of the final page of the dedication, which is reproduced by permission from the British Library copy (shelfmark 12512.aa35).

***The Amorous Abbess, or, Love in a Nunnery* (1684)**

The title page of *The Amorous Abbess* claims that the work is 'A novel, translated from the French by a woman of quality'. The novel has no preface, dedication, or introduction. The only evidence for a female translator is the title page. We have found no further evidence in support of the claim of a female translator and no evidence to the contrary.

The Amorous Abbess, or, Love in a Nunnery, set during the time 'following the Wars in Flanders' (A2r), begins in the Paris countryside with several 'Persons of Quality' at a country retreat (2). One, 'the Chevalier', receives a letter from a neglected lover, which he reads to the company. He explains the letter by narrating a story of becoming lost in a wood and being found by a local shepherd who leads him to a convent where he remains for some weeks. The Chevalier says that he hoped 'it would be the last Adventure of Knight-Errantry that would ever happen to me'. While he is in the convent, both the Abbess and her sister Egidia, a nun there, fall in love with him. As they plot to win his affections, the Chevalier falls in love with the more virtuous Egidia, and the Abbess schemes to separate them. After a failed attempt to escape from the convent with the Chevalier, Egidia takes ill and ultimately decides that they must not pursue a romantic relationship. These events are narrated by the Chevalier and another member of the retreat company, Madame d'Eyrac, who had been a visitor in the convent.

The Amorous Abbess is an English translation of part of a French novel called *Le Cercle, ou conversations galantes, histoire amoureuse du temps* (Paris 1673). Although Wing attributes *Le Cercle* to Gabriel de Brémond, the British Library catalogue gives the author as Sébastien Brémond. According to the *Dictionnaire des lettres françaises*, and to Edwin Grobe's 'Gabriel and Sébastien Brémond', the author Sébastien Brémond was confused with the travel writer Gabriel Brémond. The author of *Le Cercle* was in fact Sébastien Brémond. Born in 1645, Brémond was a refugee in Holland who wrote a number of political works, including *Hattigé*, a novel against Charles II of England, as well as amorous novels. Except for Mary Pix's *The Spanish Wives* (1696), none of Brémond's other translated works is signed by a woman. These translations include *Hattigé: or the amours of the King of Tamaran* (1680); *The apology: or, the genuine memoires of Madam Maria Manchini* (1679); *The cheating gallant* (1677); *Gallant memoirs* (1681); *The happy slave* (1677); *The princess of Montserrat* (1680); *The triumph of love over fortune* (1678); and *The victory of Catalonia* (1678). Nor have we found any evidence of female translators in unsigned translations from Brémond.

Nathaniel Noel translated *Le Cercle* into English in 1675, dedicating his translation, *The Circle: or Conversations on Love & Gallantry*, to Anne, Duchess of Monmouth. Although his translation contains more material than is included in *The Amorous Abbess*, Noel shortened his version. He claims in the Epistle to the Reader to have 'in such manner abbreviated it (though without diminishing the Matter) that it is now pleasant enough' (A5v). His translation refers to the Chevalier as the 'Cavaleer d'Estapes'. Noel includes material on the origin of the country-retreat storytelling that appears at the opening of *The Amorous Abbess*. In this episode, an abbot in the company expresses misogynist sentiments and is vehemently answered by the women in the company as well as by some of the men. Other differences between the Noel translation and *The Amorous Abbess* are limited to the brief and infrequent interruptions by the other company members, which appear in the Noel translation but are absent from *The Amorous Abbess*.

In *The Amorous Abbess* the Chevalier describes the nuns in ways that suggest anti-Catholicism. When the Chevalier is introduced to the nuns, for example, he notes that their conversation 'had not anything in it of that Monastical Air, which spoils the best things that one can say, that is infected with it' (14); the implication is that these are worldly nuns. Describing one of his many visits to the private chambers of both the Abbess and Egidia, the Chevalier remarks, 'I forgot to tell you at the beginning, that this was one of those Convents, where the Nuns enjoy a honest liberty, and where Kindred, and particular Friends are permitted to enter, and see them in their Apartments' (32). Egidia, who ends her affair with the Chevalier because she thinks it would not please God, initially confesses her love for the Chevalier by admitting that 'this day I will do more for you, then you can expect from a Woman of my humour; 'tis to confess to you, that I have much tenderness and esteem for you' (21). The Abbess is described in far more suggestive language: she 'knew so well how to rekindle flames she had once made burn, that 'twas impossible to defend one self from her' (47). The narrator seems to suggest a sexual encounter between the Chevalier and the Abbess when the latter presents herself to him in her 'Apartment … alone and undress'd' (59–60). The Chevalier describes parting from the Abbess after this encounter in the following suggestive terms: 'for a moment after I had lost sight of her I came to myself, saw my crime, and could not enough repent of it' (62). The Abbess also seems to implicate herself when she declares, 'I told her [Egidia] the Perfidiousness I had been guilty of, at which she but laught, seeing with how much freedom I confess'd it, yet she had a desire to be revenged of her Sister …' (63). When the Chevalier agrees to the Abbess's demand that he not tell Egidia of their reconciliation he remarks, 'To say truth, I owed this much, at least, to a Person that I had so great obligations to, and that had so much reason to complain of me' (77). The Abbess, remarking upon the same exchange, and in a manner unusual for her character, exclaims: 'Cruel! Thou know'st ill my heart, if thou believest I can be revenged of thee that way: I wish only that my Life were dear enough to thee, that I might punish thee by taking that away' (75).

The Amorous Abbess was published by Richard Bentley in London in 1684. Bentley published most of the English translations of Brémond's works, as well as some French originals, in Holland. A number of Bentley's editions of Brémond, including *Hattigé*, bear false imprints.

Bentley was a prolific printer who produced a wide variety of works. Some of his many publications were by women, including Marianna d'Alcoforado's *Five love-letters from a nun* (1686), Catherine Bernard's *The Count of Amboise* (1689), and Marie Catherine Aulnoy's *Memoirs of the court of France* (1692). He also published some of the novels of Mary Delarivier Manley as well as several works by Aphra Behn. In addition, Bentley was involved in the printing of many works by French authors and several anonymous works, many of which concern women or marriage.

According to librarians who have examined it for us, the British Library copy of Brémond's *Cercle* contains many English annotations in prose and verse, and the name R. Farmer is inscribed at the top of the recto of leaf two. *The Dictionary of National Biography* has an entry for an Anthony Farmer (fl. 1687) but does not note any relative whose name begins with an 'R'; *The Dictionary of National Biography Missing Persons* and *Women and the DNB* also fail to note an R. Farmer. Although not all of the annotations have been recorded, those of which we are aware are brief summaries, such as 'Of love' and 'How a lady may know true from false lovers: & how receive a declaration of love'.

In addition to the British Library copy of the 1684 edition of *The Amorous Abbess* (shelfmark 12410.c22) reproduced in this volume, another copy, too tightly bound for reproduction, is held at UCLA. *The National Union Catalog Pre-1956 Imprints* lists an edition printed in 1748 in Dublin by A. Long.

***Peppa, or the reward of constant love a novel: done out of French: with several songs set to musick for two voices / by a young-gentlewoman* (1689)**

Peppa is anonymous except for the initials 'A. C.'. at the end of the dedication. The evidence for female authorship is found on the title page, which calls the author a 'young Gentlewoman', and in the dedication, in which A. C. uses a female pronoun to refer to herself: 'One Favour more I importunely crave, that for some Reasons (which by you, Madam, shall be commanded from me at any time,) I may be permitted to refrain the publishing my Name in Print; tho really nothing is so sensible a Grief to me, as that I am forc'd to stifle my greatest Ambition, which is, to declare to the World, the Name of *her*, who, among all the Crowd of your Admirers, is the most zealously, / Madam, / Your Honour's / Most Humble, / Most Faithful, / And most devoted Servant, / A. C.' (A5v–A6v; emphasis added).

The Bodleian Library copy of *Peppa* has a note in a nineteenth-century hand: 'by Lady Cokaine'. The Beinecke Library also suggests this attribution in its catalogue record. According to the Bodleian, a bookseller's catalogue notes that Sir Aston Cokaine's wife was Mary, daughter of Sir Gilbert Knyveton, but that the signature 'A. C.' may refer to Aston Cokaine (also spelled Cokain and Cokayne). Cokaine (1608–1684) published several translations, poems, and dramatic works. We have found no other evidence proving or disproving the claims of authorship for either Aston or Mary Cokaine. The Beinecke Library copy of *Peppa* also has the words 'Mary Fielford' written on the title page, but the library considers this to be an early ownership statement rather than an attribution. We have not found other information about Fielford. The OCLC record notes that this copy also has a book-stamp of Alfred Wallis.

The only secondary source reference to *Peppa* that we have located is R. I. Le Tellier's comment in *The English Novel, 1660–1700: an annotated bibliography* that he does not believe that *Peppa* is a translation: it 'purports to be an trn [sic] from French, but seems an original work' (343). Le Tellier does not provide any evidence for this claim.

Peppa is set in Genoa, in the household of Prince Mark Antony Doria and his daughter Peppa. Peppa is raised by her aunt, the Marchioness Durazzo, because her mother died while giving birth to her and her father retired to a monastery to recover from the loss of his wife. Eventually Doria marries Lady Spinola, and the novel opens with Peppa's return to her father's household along with her cousin Julia, from whom she could not bear to part. Lady Spinola wants Peppa to marry her nephew, the Marquess Spinola, in order to strengthen the ties between their two houses (Lady Spinola is unable to bear children). Peppa, however, falls in love with the 'French Chevalier of _____', whom she encounters at a carnival during which the Marquess Spinola intends to make public his feelings for her. The Chevalier instantly falls in love with Peppa and composes two sonnets set to music in honour of his beloved.

By the end of the novel Peppa and the Chevalier marry, but only after overcoming several obstacles. Because the Chevalier is called back to France after the carnival, he and Peppa reveal their love for one another through an exchange of letters facilitated by the Chevalier's friend Count Centurione. One of Peppa's letters is mistakenly delivered to the Marquess Spinola, rather than to the

Count, and the letter is revealed to Lady Spinola. The Marquess Spinola mistakes Centurione for Peppa's suitor and, after losing a duel to him, leaves Genoa to escape his shame. Centurione marries Peppa's cousin Julia and continues to deliver letters to Peppa from the Chevalier. This unexpected union leads Lady Spinola to believe that the intercepted love letter was Julia's letter to Centurione, rather than Peppa's to the Chevalier, and so she calls for the return of her nephew.

Peppa's father in the meantime chooses a new husband for Peppa, the Spaniard Villa Mediana Celi, a match that gains the approval of the Spanish king. The Spaniard's vanity causes him to spread false rumours in Spain of his 'success' with Peppa, who in fact is repelled by him (72). Peppa's father becomes privy to these rumours and in an attempt to verify them asks Peppa to speak openly to him about her passion. Peppa, who thinks her father has discovered her feelings for the Chevalier, admits to being in love with someone and her partial admission incenses Doria, who misinterprets it as confirmation of the lascivious reports of the Spaniard. Doria temporarily falls ill from the thought of his daughter's promiscuity; Peppa mistakenly attributes her father's illness to his disappointment that she has chosen a Frenchman over a Spaniard.

Peppa's stepmother, Lady Spinola, conspires with her nephew to stage a false kidnapping to prevent Peppa from continuing her romance and to allow the Marquess Spinola to rescue her and thus win her affection. The kidnapping takes place, but the Chevalier unknowingly preempts Spinola by rescuing Peppa and Lady Spinola, thus permanently securing Peppa's affections. Lady Spinola relates her failure to Peppa's father, who in turn accepts the Spaniard's continuing requests to marry Peppa, a match that would be both politically expedient and materially profitable for Doria. At this point in the story, Italy goes to war against France and Doria sends his family to Turin for protection. Peppa hears a report of the death of a chevalier in Genoa and fears it is her lover. She confesses her love for the Chevalier to Lady Spinola, who is moved by her story and, discovering that Peppa's lover was not the deceased chevalier, reunites them. In the end they are married with the consent of the French king and Peppa's parents.

The original French text and its author are unknown. *Peppa* is dedicated 'To the Honourable the Lady Isabella Roberts'. We have located no biographical information about Roberts. The author says only that Roberts has favoured her in the past, 'and relying upon that alone, I beg this one favour more, your Patronage, and Acceptance of the Virgin Essay, the Product of my Leisure Hours' (A3r–v).

Peppa was printed in 1689 in London for William Crooke, a printer and bookseller from 1667 to 1694; a sample of the works he published can be seen in the catalogue of titles he appended to *Peppa*. The title page of *Peppa* also indicates that the novel was licensed in 1689 by James Fraser, who also licensed many political works, including Daniel Defoe's *Reflections upon the late great revolution* (1689).

In addition to the fine Beinecke Rare Book Library (Yale University) copy of *Peppa* reproduced here, copies of *Peppa* are held at the Bodleian Library, The British Library, and the Library of Congress.

Alcander and Philocrates: Or, The Pleasures and Disquietudes of Marriage. A Novel. Written by a Young Lady (1696)

The evidence for female authorship of *Alcander and Philocrates* consists of the title-page's claim that it was 'Written by a Young Lady' and the dedicatory epistle, in which the author asks the dedicatee, James Douglas, Earl of Arran, not to be 'too severe on a Woman's Faults' (3). We have not located any independent source that confirms or disputes the female authorship of the novel. At the end of the dedication, the author writes that she has protected herself from the 'vain Censures of the Town' by writing under the protection of the dedicatee's name and by allowing herself to be 'known by no Name' (4). Although the author calls the work a 'Trifle' and a 'mean present', and says that she aims to write something 'less unworthy' in the future, she does not apologize for writing and publishing even though these acts could still be considered inappropriate for women (1). She also proclaims her intention of producing a second work, one that will require greater 'Genius' (3).

The dedicatee, James Douglas, Earl of Arran, later fourth Duke of Hamilton (1658–1712) was appointed by Charles II as ambassador to Louis XIV in 1683, remained in France until 1685 and fought in two of Louis's campaigns. He supported James II in the revolution of 1688 and was sent to the Tower upon the arrival of William of Orange at Whitehall. Arran was released in April 1689, but then imprisoned for more than a year on suspicion of corresponding with the French court; after his release, he retired back to Scotland. In 1696 (the year in which *Alcander and Philocrates* was published), he reappeared in England to surrender on a warrant for conspiracy and was acquitted without a trial. In 1698 his mother, Anne, Duchess of Hamilton, resigned her honours, by permission of the king, in favour of her son, who was created Duke of Hamilton, Marquis of Clydesdale, &c. Arran married twice, first Lady Anne Spencer, eldest daughter of Robert, Earl of Sunderland, who died in 1690 without surviving children, and then, in 1698, Elizabeth, only child and heiress of Digby, Lord Gerard. In the interval between marriages Arran fathered a son (Charles Hamilton, 1695–1754) with Lady Barbara Fitzroy (1672–1737), third daughter of Charles II and his mistress Barbara Villiers, Duchess of Cleveland.

We have found no evidence to explain the choice of Arran as the novel's dedicatee, but the tone of the dedication, coupled with Arran's circumstances at the time of its publication, raises the possibility that the author intended to offer a subtle criticism of Arran as well as praise. The dedication of *Alcander and Philocrates*, a novel that features a debate over the value of marriage for men, to the Earl of Arran may be interpreted in light of Arran's fathering an illegitimate child. The author implies in the dedication that the Earl's positive prior experience in marriage will assure his choice in favor of marriage when he reads of the novel's debate:

> your Lordship, who has try'd both Estates, will be best able to give a just Sentence; [line cropped off top of page] of the Countess of Arran, will not doubt for which side you will determine; a Lady, so perfectly accomplish'd _____ but I dare not attempt to praise her, whose Name, ought to be celebrated by all the noblest Pens, if her own Vertues did not give her a more certain Immortality. (1–2)

The author's assumption of Arran's favorable disposition toward marriage suggests her support of a second marriage for Arran. The dedication emphasizes that only a second marriage would fulfill 'our Expectations' for 'a young Inheritor of the Glory and Dignity of his great Ancestors, and of those Noble Vertues, which give your Lordship a more venerable Greatness than that which you derive from your illustrious Birth' (2).

As in many early novels, the names of characters in this work are possibly coded. There may be a clue to the author's view of Arran in the name Alcander, which circulated widely in classical and early modern literature. Among its various resonances, the name (in part from the Greek word for man, *andro*) primarily served either to praise a heroic man or to criticize a lascivious man. The name is also found in various classical and contemporary works. In the works of Homer, Virgil and Ovid, Alcander figures as an otherwise unidentified slain warrior. In Plutarch's *Lycurgus: The Father of Sparta*, Alcander is a violent youth who eventually becomes one of the best citizens of Sparta. The figure Alcandro appears briefly in Tasso's *Gerusalemme Liberata* (1581, English trans. 1600); he is the elder son of Ardelio, who is killed by Clorinda. In Anne Finch's play *Aristomenes: Or, The Royal Shepherd* (1713), Alcander is a soldier who has been ordered to marshal a battle, while in two of her poems he figures as a constant lover. In Sarah Fyge's 'The Repulse to Alcander' (1703), however, Alcander is represented as a 'lewd Abuse[r]' who makes advances toward a married woman. Initially the woman tries to excuse his inappropriate behaviour, but since he seems emboldened by her silence she chooses to announce publicly her 'scorn' for his 'Amours', and to denounce his 'Vanity and Pride' in an attempt to 'shun at once the Censure and the Crime' (ll. 25–27).

Whether the choice of the name Alcander for one of the novel's protagonists is original to *Alcander and Philocrates* or derives from a source text used as inspiration for the tale, the author may be connecting the name's literary connotations to Arran's marital and personal history. Moreover, Louis XIV, whom Arran served and supported, was known as the 'Great Alcander'. Louis was notorious for the excesses of his court, epitomized in the building of Versailles and his numerous mistresses. In 1680, however, responding to the

Affair of the Poisons, a scandal resulting from the dissolute nature of his court, Louis renounced pleasure and embraced piety. This decision led to the termination of his affair with the Marquise de Montespan and his association with the pious Madame de Maintenon, whom he married in 1684 after the death of the Queen. Louis's decision to marry can be interpreted as part of his return to piety. By alluding to Louis XIV through the choice of the name Alcander for the character opposed to marriage, the author of *Alcander and Philocrates* may have sought to emphasize the desirability of marriage for Arran, in contrast to his current immoral behaviour.

The novel's protagonists, Alcander and Philocrates, hold opposing views on marriage. When Philocrates intends to marry his beloved Fraudelisa, Alcander begins a verbal crusade to dissuade him. Despite his defence of the fidelity and virtue of his own beloved, Lesbia, Alcander opposes marriage on the grounds that women are incomprehensible, insincere, and 'change without reason [and] have no solidity in their Wit, or in their Heart' (5–6). Philocrates, in contrast, argues that a man will not marry a woman whom he does not know to be worthy and virtuous, and such a woman will help her husband maintain these qualities in himself. Rather than continue the debate among themselves, Alcander and Philocrates appoint their friend the Abbot Sophin to judge the merit of their respective arguments. At the Abbot's direction, Alcander and Philocrates observe several married couples in Paris, yet each remains undeterred in his convictions.

As the tale unfolds, readers discover that both men have been deceived by the women they love. Although troubled by the behaviour of Fraudelisa and Lesbia, Alcander and Philocrates come to accept the women's carefully devised excuses, which have been constructed with the help of a widow whom they meet and entrust with their stories while seeking temporary refuge in a convent. Near the end of the tale, Alcander and Philocrates both tell the abbot of their intentions to marry and ask his advice. The abbot subtly mocks them for believing the artifices of women and concludes that a man's constitution should be the basis for determining whether he should marry. Realizing, though, that the men will not leave without his blessing, he grudgingly accepts their unions with the following stipulations:

I don't advise you to Marriage (he said addressing himself to Alcander) if you find in your self a Vertue firm and constant enough to sanctifie you in a perfect Continence: I don't forbid it you continued he, [(] turning to Philocrates) if you find it necessary for the Good, and Repose of your Conscience; but know both of you, that for what concerns the Choice of that State of Life, as of all others, we ought to look upon no other Consideration, and direct our Conduct but by that alone (132).

The abbot's approval of marriage gets lost in the verbosity of his response. While seemingly revealing what consideration a man should ultimately rely on when contemplating marriage, he instead neglects to offer this insight to Alcander and Philocrates, thus leaving them to their own devices: 'we ought to look upon no other [unspecified] Consideration'. Our impression of the abbot's response and of the novel's conclusion is that the decision of a man to marry is both personal and optional—a position with which the author appears to disagree in the preface, and which she relies on Arran to correct by appointing him the final adjudicator of the text's dispute over marriage.

While the dedication does not clarify the question of authorship, the language of the dedicatory epistle does raise the question of whether this work is original:

And I was the more willing to throw this little Book at your Lordships Feet, that the shame of having made your Lordship so mean a Present may incite me to some more noble Undertaking, by way of atonement; and the Ambition of producing something *of my own*, less unworthy of your Lordship's Protection, may inspire me beyond my natural Genius. (1; emphasis added)

The phrase 'of my own' may mean 'in my own name' or might imply that this tale does not originate with the author of the dedication. *Alcander and Philocrates* could be an original work, an unacknowledged translation, or a rewriting of a popular tale, so that the words are hers but the plot another's. Evidence that the narrative is in some respect not the creation of the author may also be seen in her request to Arran to settle the dispute between Alcander and Philocrates, who she believes had 'chosen a very improper, because an unexperienc'd Judge of their Contest' in the Abbot Sophin (3). Her dissatisfaction with the outcome of the novel may indicate that the ending is not her own.

Alcander and Philocrates was published in London by Richard Parker, Samuel Briscoe, and Samuel Burrowes in 1696. Parker, a bookseller and publisher of plays and historical works from 1692 to 1725, published two other works by women: Catherine Cockburn's *Agnes de Castro* (1696) and Anne de La Roche-Guilhem's *Zingis* (1692). Briscoe, a bookseller from 1691 to 1700, was the publisher of many of Aphra Behn's works. Plomer's *Dictionary* identifies Samuel Burrowes as a London bookseller, 1697 to 1707. His name appears only on *Alcander and Philocrates* and a Latin textbook.

Wing does not list any subsequent editions of *Alcander and Philocrates*, and only one tightly bound copy is extant. That copy, at the University of Illinois at Urbana-Champaign, is reprinted in this volume. We thank Professors Alvan Bregman and Bruce Swann of the Rare Book and Special Collections Library at the University of Illinois at Urbana-Champaign for their assistance in securing reproducible copies of many problem pages. The title page bears the name 'N Fox', which may be an early ownership signature. Several undecipherable handwritten words also appear on pages 16, 17, and 35. The only modern edition of *Alcander and Philocrates* that we have located is the Chadwyck-Healey machine-readable transcript in the Early English Prose Fiction Full-Text Database (1997).

References

Wing C412 [*Diotrephe*]; Wing A3017 [*Amorous*]; Wing P1448 [*Peppa*]; Wing A884A [*Alcander*]

Arber, Edward (1903–6), *The Term Catalogues, 1668–1709*, vol. II: 70, rpt. [1965], New York: Johnson Reprint Corporation

Bell, Maureen, George Parfitt and Simon Shepherd (eds) (1990), *A Biographical Dictionary of English Women Writers, 1580 – 1720*, Boston: G.K. Hall

Blain, Virginia, Patricia Clements and Isobel Grundy (1990), *The Feminist Companion to Literature in English*, New Haven, CT: Yale University Press

Brémond, Sébastien (1673), *Le Cercle, ou conversations galantes*, Paris

Camus, Jean-Pierre (1626), *Diotrephe: Histoire Valentine*, Lyon: Antoine Chard

Clancy, Rev. Thomas (1996), *English Catholic Books, 1641–1700*, Brookfield, VT: Scolar Press

Courtilz de Sandras, Gatien (1684), *Les Conquêtes Amoureuses du Grand Alcandre dans les Pays-Bas*. Translated as (1685) *The amorous conquests of the great Alcander or, The amours of the French king and Madam Montespan*, London: Printed by R. Bentley and S. Magnes

— (1686), *Les Dames dans leur Naturel ou la Galantrie sans façon sous le règne du Grand Alcandre*

— (1696), *Le Grand Alcandre Frustré*, Cologne: P. Marteau

Dictionnaire de lettres françaises, vol. 3 (1994), Paris: Fayard

Du Verger, S. (1639), *Admirable Events*, rpt. ed. Jane Collins (1996), *The Early Modern Englishwoman: A Facsimile Library of Essential Works*, Part I, vol. 5, Aldershot, England: Scolar Press

Du Vergers Humble Reflections (1657), London

Egerton, Sarah Fyge (1703), *Poems on Several Occasions, Together with a Pastoral*, London: Printed and sold by J. Nutt

Esdaile, Arundell James (1970), *A List of English tales and prose romances printed before 1740*, New York: B. Franklin

Finch, Anne Kingsmill, Countess of Winchilsea (1713), *Miscellany Poems on Several Occasions*, London: Printed for John Barber

Grobe, Edwin (1963), 'Gabriel and Sébastien Brémond', *Romance Notes*, 4:2, 132–5

Hunter, J. Paul (1990), *Before Novels: The cultural contexts of eighteenth-century English fiction*, New York: Norton

Le Tellier, Robert Ignatius (1997), *The English Novel, 1660–1700: an annotated bibliography*, Westport, CT: Greenwood Press

Mish, Charles Carroll (1967), *English prose fiction, 1600–1700: a chronological checklist*, Charlottesville, VA: Bibliographical Society of the University of Virginia

Noel, Nathaniel (1675), *The Circle: Or Conversations on Love & Gallantry*, London: Printed for the Author, and are to be sold by John Carre, Richard Hunt, and George Miller

Plomer, Henry (1907), *A Dictionary of the Printers and Booksellers Who Were at Work in England, Scotland and Ireland from 1641 to 1667*, London: Bibliographical Society

— (1968), *A Dictionary of the Booksellers and Printers Who Were at Work in England, Scotland and Ireland from 1668 to 1725*, London: Bibliographical Society

Prynne, William (1646), *Diotrephes Catechised*, London: Printed for Michael Sparke

Simpson, J. A. and E. S. C. Weiner (1989), *The Oxford English Dictionary*, Oxford: Clarendon Press

Stephen, Sir Leslie and Sir Sidney Lee (eds) (1963–5), *Dictionary of National Biography*, London: Oxford University Press

Trill, Suzanne; Kate Chedgzoy and Melanie Osborne (eds) (1997), *Lay By Your Needles Ladies, Take the Pen*, London: Arnold

Udall, John (1588), *The State of the Church of Englande, Laide Open in a conference betweene Diotrephes a bishop, Tertullus a papist, Demetrius an usurer, Pandocheus an in-keeper, and Paule a preacher of the word of God*, London: R. Waldegrave

Watson, George, ed. (1969–1977), *The New Cambridge Bibliography of English Literature*, vol. 2, Cambridge: Cambridge University Press

Womock, Laurence (1661), *The Result of False Principles*, London: Printed for William Leake

Woodbridge, Benjamin (1916), '*Le Grand Alcandre Frustré* and *La Princesse de Clèves*', *The Modern Language Review*, 11:4, 409–419

Peppa:

Weyypa

OR,

The REWARD

OF

CONSTANT LOVE.

A

NOVEL.

𝕯𝖔𝖓𝖊 𝖔𝖚𝖙 𝖔𝖋 French.

With feveral SONGS fet to MU-
SICK, for TWO VOICES.

By a Young-Gentlewoman.

Licenfed, 1689.
JAMES FRASER

LONDON,
Printed for *William Crooke* at the *Green*
Dragon without *Temple-Bar.* 1689.

PEPPA:

OR, THE

REWARD

OF

CONSTANT LOVE.

GEnoa is a City of *Italy*, not lefs famous for its Antiqui-ty than for the flourifhing Condition it is in at pre-fent, maintain'd chiefly by a Commerce, and good Correfpondence with almoft all the Nations of the Uni-verfe; and is now efteem'd one of the richeft Towns in *Europe*.

As this City is very Ancient, fo there is in it many Illuftrious Families, and fome that are allied to Soveraign Princes, amongft whom, the Prince

B   *Mark*

Mark Antony Doria made no small Figure, being in as great esteem for his vast Riches and Possessions, as for the Nobility of his Ancestors; and having an earnest desire in these latter Times, to make the Glory of his Family shine out in his own Person, he apply'd his youthful Time and Courage, for some years, in the Service of the *Spaniard*; but not meeting with those Honourable Rewards which his Courage had merited, he discontentedly retir'd to *Genoa*; where, some little time after, he married the Sister of the Marquess *Durazzo*, a person of an exquisite Beauty. All People look'd upon this Marriage as very happy, seeing the assiduous care the Prince *Doria* took to please his Wife, who in requital lov'd him with an extream Passion. About a year after they were married, she was deliver'd of a Daughter; but her lying in was follow'd with a Consequence so fatal, that tho all means were us'd, she relaps'd into a great weakness of Body, and, after having languish'd five or six Months, dy'd. The Prince was so sensibly touch'd with this loss, that he withdrew himself for a long time into a Monastery, without seeing any body, avoiding even those

very

very perfons who were only capable of
giving him fome Comfort. The little
Princefs, who was nam'd *Peppa*, was
brought up under the Tuition of her
Aunt the Marchionefs *Durazzo*, who
had a Daughter of the fame age. The
Prince *Doria* led a life very retir'd for
four years, not endering to hear of a
fecond Marriage; neverthelefs his Relations and Friends did urge him with
fuch preffing Arguments, that having
at length determin'd to give them fatisfaction, he courted a Lady of the
Houfe of *Spinola*. It was not long before he married her, but fhe had never
the fortune to be with Child; fo that
Peppa, who in her tender Infancy had
already the marks of a perfect Beauty,
was look'd upon as one of the greateft
Fortunes of all *Italy*.

The Princefs *Doria*, now after a feven
years Marriage, defpairing ever to give
her Husband a Succeffour, found fome
Comfort in thinking, that fhe might
one day unite the two Houfes of *Doria*
and *Spinola*, by the Marriage of the
young Marquefs *Spinola* her Nephew
with *Peppa*; and to the end that fhe
might have the opportunity of preparing betimes the Mind of *Peppa*, fhe ear-

B 2   neftly

neftly entreated her Husband to recall his Daughter into his own Houfe, affuring him, that fhe had an extream affection for her, and that fhe did now look upon *Peppa* as her own Child. The Prince *Doria* lov'd his Daughter moft entirely, was in an extafy of joy to underftand the defire of his Wife, and did not delay the fatisfaction which fhe defir'd.

Peppa was receiv'd into her Father's Houfe with all the Teftimonies of Love and Affection that fhe could expect from a Mother-in-law, who would be no longer fuch towards her, for fhe defir'd her Husband to let *Peppa* call her Mother; and fhe would give her the name of Daughter. *Peppa*, who was of a fine Wit, anfwer'd with an obliging readinefs to all the kindneffes exprefs'd to her by her Mother-in-law. The Princefs on her fide did whatever fhe thought would pleafe her Daughter-in-law; and being inform'd that *Peppa* was much troubl'd to part with one of her Coufins which fhe lov'd entirely; fhe intreated the Marchionefs *Durazzo*, to permit her Daughter *Julia* to be bred with *Peppa* in the Family of the Prince *Doria*. The Marchionefs, who had many

ny Children, and could not maintain
them according to their Quality, had
defign'd them Nuns. 'Twas for this
reafon, that with much difficulty fhe
was brought to yield, that *Julia* fhould
live with her Coufin. Neverthelefs *Peppa*
pa wifh'd it with fo much eagernefs, and
her Relations, who had a great deal of
kindnefs for her, fo earneftly defir'd
this of the Marchionefs, that fhe no
longer oppos'd it. *Peppa* and *Julia* fuffer'd not the difpleafure of being parted, and the delights of living always
together, contributed ftill further to the
ftrengthening that perfect Union which
was between them. The Princefs *Do-*
ria, who had her Intereft in profpect,
let flip no opportunity of entertaining
Peppa with the Grandure of the Houfe
of *Spinola*, the famous Captains that it
hath produc'd for the Honour of *Italy*,
and a great many advantages confiderable that it had above the other Families
of *Genoa*. She added, that fhe was
much deceiv'd if the young Marquefs
Spinola, who had already a delicate
Meen, and a great deal of Wit, did not
maintain with Splendor, the Glory of
his Anceftours. *Peppa* liften'd to the
difcourfe of the Princefs, without making

the leaſt Reflection ; but in the end perceiving that they made the Marqueſs of *Spinola* be more than ordinary aſſiduous, in rendring her his Devoirs, and that her Mother-in-law, cunningly ingag'd to make now and then Appointments of Diverſions with the Marqueſs, ſhe complain'd to *Julia* of this conſtraint of her Humour, finding her ſelf only pleas'd when ſhe was in her company ; and all the means that the Princeſs *Doria* us'd made *Peppa* have the greater averſion for the Marqueſs.

In the mean while, tho *Peppa* was yet but fourteen years old, all that ſaw her, ſpoke of her Beauty with admiration ſhe was of a fine ſhape, the Features of her Face were very delicate, curious Eyes, a fine Skin, and ſhe had ſomething in her Face that was ſo taking, that it was impoſſible to look on her without having an infinite eſteem for her perſon.

Julia was not ſo perfect Beauty, but ſhe had much Spritelineſs, and not a little Sweetneſs appear'd in the whole Cymetry of her Face. She would ſometimes ſay to her Couſin, That ſhe was of a different Humour from all other young Maids, who are always troubled that

that they are not handsome enough
whereas nothing discompos'd her more
than to hear the World say she had
Beauty; for had she been depriv'd of it,
she could have quitted the World without any Regret, and past the rest of her
life in a Convent, as she was design'd.
Peppa endeavour'd to comfort her, by
letting her know, that she was not
made for the Cloister, and that something might happen which would cause a
change in the Will of her Parents.

The fame of *Peppa's* Beauty was carried over all *Italy*, and that she was the
only Heiress to the House of *Doria*. All
these reasons oblig'd several Persons of
eminent Quality to esteem the Possession
of her to be a Fortune that would
crown their utmost desire. There was
one, even a Soveraign Prince, who defir'd her for his Son, but the Princess
Doria rais'd secretly so many difficulties, that the business was at last broke
off. The Marquess *Spinola*, who found
Peppa very agreeable, and perceiv'd the
great advantages that would accrue to
him by this Alliance, made it his whole
study to please her; and now through
his own Inclination he began really to
love her, who till then had but seemingly

done it, out of compliance to his Relations. He perceiv'd that *Peppa* was not in
the leaft touch'd with his Love, which
made him refolve to try, whether he
could not take the advantage of the
Carnaval-time, for to give to his Miftrefs the moft publick marks of the
Paffion he had for her. This *Carnaval*
is a time of Rejoicing, (or rather, mad
Frolicks) in moft Countries of *Europe*,
(efpecially among the *Romanifts*), and
lafts from *Chriftmas* till *Shrove-Tuefday*
at night, at which time their madnefs
ends; for which, during the *Lent*,
they feem to do Penance : This is fomething agreeable to an old *Englifh* Pro-
verb; *Sweet Meats will have fower Sauce.*
But to return to our Marquefs, he came
to all the Balls with a magnificent Appearance. There he danc'd feveral
times with *Peppa* ; and when fhe retir'd,
he took care that feveral Violins fhould
always attend her Coach to the Door,
and there ftay the greateft part of the
night. Neverthelefs, as all things feem
infipid to a perfon that has no Taft,
Peppa made no returns to his preffing So-
licitations, and acknowledg'd to *Julia*,
in private, that fhe did not find her felf
at all difpos'd to receive Addreffes from
the

the Marquefs, and that fhe well forefaw, fhe fhould be the moft unhappy perfon in the World, if her Parents did oblige her to marry him.

The *Chevalier* of——— and another *French* Gentleman, by chance happen'd to be at *Genoa* during this *Carnaval*, and going to feveral Balls in Mafquerade, as being the Cuftom of the Country; they, hearing that there was to be at the Palace of the Marquefs *Juftiniano* a great Feaft, which was to be concluded with a Ball, were refolv'd to go thither, difguis'd in the form of Sea-Monfters. It being an unufual fort of Mafquerade, every one was ftrangely furpris'd to fee a fpectacle fo extraordinary, and which frighten'd fome of the Ladies ; the two Gentlemen perceiving it, they untied only a fmall ftring, by the help whereof they flipp'd cut of their monftrous Habit, and appear'd extreamly gallant. The *Chevalier* of——— was one of the handfomeft Men in the World, and his fhape was not lefs admirable, which attracted the Eyes of all that were prefent. They both danc'd with a very good Grace, and particularly the *Chevalier*, that the other Gentlemen durft fcarce dance after him. All the Affembly re-

main'd not a little fatisfy'd, crowning
them with all the Applaufe imaginable.
The *Chevalier* of—— having obferv'd
that *Peppa* and *Julia* were in difcourfe
with two other Ladies, went and plac'd
himfelf by them. The Ladies gave him
infinite praifes, affuring him, that they
never faw a Man fo gentilely habited,
nor that danc'd fo finely. The *Chevalier*
anfwer'd very modeftly to all their Com-
pliments, but with a great deal of Wit.
The Ladies, who knew him not, and
were ignorant even of what Nation he
was, becaufe he fpoke very well their
Language, were very curious of his
Acquaintance. They had all no fmall
refpect for his Perfon, and the more he
utter'd any thing that charm'd thefe Ladies, the more their Curiofity encreas'd:
At laft it came to that, that they defir'd
him to take off his Mask for a moment.
The *Chevalier*, who was fatisfy'd that
they did not know him, had the Complaifance to do what they defir'd, and let
them fee a Face, which if difagreeing
with the reft of his perfon, was only
fo by being too handfome. He put
on his Mask again not long after, and
remain'd fome time converfing with
them. He obferv'd *Peppa* very attentively,

tively, and thought her the moſt beautiful Creature that he had ever ſeen.
He began to take a great delight in being near her, and was juſt about examining all the Features of her Face, when
the Marqueſs *Spinola* came to deſire her
to dance. *Peppa*, who was in diſcourſe
with the *Chevalier*, and not a little
pleas'd with it, was ſo troubled at the
Marqueſs's Compliment, that, tho ſhe
roſe to give him her Hand, ſhe ſcarce
knew what ſhe did; and ſhe had not
danc'd long before ſhe was ſeiz'd with
ſuch a Faintneſs, that forc'd her to
quit the Ball before it was ended. The
Chevalier of —— went out preſently after, and the next morning went aboard
his own Veſſel to return to *France*,
where he diſcours'd to all his Friends of
the charming Creature that he had ſeen
at *Genoa*; he himſelf wondring at the
ſame time, how he could command
himſelf ſo far as to leave her, and take
a Reſolution of departing. Notwithſtanding, as he was no leſs skilful in
Muſick and Poetry, than in the Dance,
he had not the power to withſtand
ſome ſoft moments, wherein he com-
pos'd ſeveral Sonnets in praiſe of the
fair *Peppa*; among which here is one.

When.

W
Hen Phillis *first* I *saw*, *that*

lovely Maid, how great was my sur-

prise: She in a moment did my Heart

invade, wi'th' Magick of her Eyes:

She in a moment did my Heart invade,

wi'th'

wi'th' *Magick of her Eyes*; wi'th'

Magick of her Eyes.

2.

Approach I did, but with so great an Awe,
I trembling speechless stood:
Unusual heat did all my Veins o'reflow,
Then chill'd was all my Blood.
Unusual, *&c.*

3.

Confusion did my Resolution bind,
Scarce could I speak, or move:
Despair had took possession of my Mind
And check'd my hopes of Love.
Despair, *&c.*

As

As foon as *Peppa* was alone with her Coufin, fhe unbofom'd her thoughts to her, and declar'd, That fhe would never pardon the Marquefs *Spinola* the fenfible difpleafure he had done her, by his interrupting the Converfation which they had with the Stranger, whom they found fo obliging. *Have you ever feen,* continu'd *Peppa,* a *Man fo handfome, that had fo fine a Wit, and fo agreeable, and that danc'd with fuch a Majeftick Air? If we had difcours'd longer with him,* interrupted *Julia, we might perhaps have difcover'd who he was. I muft needs own,* cry'd *Peppa,* blufhing, *the fight of him has made no fmall impreffion in my Thoughts, and not to make any further fecret of it between us, I cann't but acknowledge, that ever fince that time I have felt fuch emotions, whereof till then I was wholly ignorant. In the mean time I don't know him, neither can I tell the Country he is of, and perhaps we fhall never fee him more.* Thefe laft words were ended with a figh, which difcover'd, that this Stranger was not indifferent to her, and altho her Coufin gave her fome hopes that fhe might meet him at another Ball, yet this hope was too weak to bring her much Comfort. Thefe

two

two Ladies met at almoſt all the diverting Paſtimes that were perform'd at Genoa, during the time of the Carnaval.
Peppa, who found not what ſhe look'd
for, was always in a Melancholy Humour, and complain'd ſtill to her Couſin of her bad Fortune. She ſometimes
oblig'd her to keep her company the
greateſt part of the day at the Window,
where they could ſee all that paſt by,
without being ſeen by any, flattering
her ſelf, that ſhe might at laſt ſee him,
who was now become the ſole object of
her Thoughts. But notwithſtanding
all this trouble for a whole month, it
was to very little purpoſe, ſince that the
Chevalier of——— was now in France,
where all his Eſtate and Fortune lay.

The Count Centurione of Genoa, who
had been acquainted with him in Italy,
happening to be at Paris, after his return
from a Voyage in Germany, was overjoy'd to find the Chevalier there. He
went to ſee him, and was receiv'd with
a great deal of kindneſs. It was not a-
bove two days after that the Count was
in a troubleſome Affair with an Engliſh
Gentleman. They fought, and the
Engliſh Gentleman was much wounded ;
but the greateſt danger was, that they
were

were both feiz'd, and as none doubted but that it was a Duel, (which Crime in *France* finds no Favour) their Trial came on. The *Chevalier*, who was advertis'd of it, by a Note from *Centuriani*, took this Affair in hand, but foreseeing that they could not escape being convicted, and that his Friend thereby would run the hazard of losing his Head, he thought it not convenient to endeavour any thing from the Judges, who, he knew, lay under indispensable obligations of proceeding to give Sentence according to Evidence; but having understood, that they who saw the Action were People of a mean Quality, he privately search'd them out, and by great Rewards oblig'd them to steal out of *Paris*, so that there might be none to witness against his Friend. This took the desir'd effect, for the Judges finding no proof against him that was valid, were forc'd to acquit him. *Centurione* out of acknowledgment for this generous proceeding of his Friend, would have made him a considerable Present; but the *Chevalier* refus'd it, assuring him, that he was fully recompens'd for that care he took to bring his Affair to a happy end, by the Plea-

sure

sure he receiv'd in being serviceable to a
person of his worth. The Count *Centurione* return'd back into his own Country full of grateful Acknowledgments
for the generous Action of his Deliverer,
having always before his Eyes the obligations that lay on him for so signal a
piece of Service.

In the mean while, the great Discourse at *Genoa*, was of the Marriage of
the Marquess *Spinola* with *Peppa*, it being look'd upon as a thing agreed on
between the two Families. The Princess *Doria*, who most passionately defir'd it, press'd several times her Bro-
ther, and her Husband, to procure a
meeting of their Relations, to make an
end of regulating all matters : But *Peppa*, who was always full of the Idea of
her Stranger, and who, not seeing
which way to evade this Marriage,
which she now was afraid would be too
certain, fell into a languishing illness,
which equally put a stop to the Design
of both Houses ; so that they deferr'd
their meeting to seal the Articles to a
longer time. The Physicians, tho they
were ignorant of *Peppa*'s Distemper,
prescrib'd her several things , and
through their Advice, she was carried
to.

to a Countrey-House, which the Prince
Doria had at *Sancto P. di Arena*, for a
change of Air. *Julia*, who alone could
administer any Comfort to her, because
she knew her Secrets, did in vain represent, that she fill'd her Thoughts
with the Idea of a Man, whom probably she should never see again, and
blam'd her infinitely for resisting her
Father's Will, who would make sure to
her his whole Estate, upon her Marriage with the Marquess *Spinola*. *Peppa*
rested satisfy'd with the Reasons alledg'd by her Cousin; but at the same
time affirm'd, That 'twas impossible to
alter her Mind, and to drive from her
Thoughts the Image of her dear Stranger.

The illness of *Peppa* caus'd so much
trouble in the Mind of the Marquess *Spinola*, who now really lov'd her, that
his Relations thought it fit to dissipate
his too great care for his Mistress, that
he should go and see most of the chief
Towns that were in *Italy*. Of this *Peppa* was soon inform'd: And as it would
prolong the Marriage, it became a matter of great Consolation, and from
that moment she grew better, and began to shake off her Distemper : *Julia*
forgot

forgot nothing that might divert her,
and perceiving that she did not speak
so often to her of her Stranger, there
having been almost two years gone
without hearing any news of him, she
instantly begg'd, that now she would
banish from her Mind, that fatal Idea,
and consider, that the happiness of her
Person, and of two Illustrious Houses
depended solely upon her own Will,
since it was in her power to be the hap-
piest person in *Italy*, and to taste
the greatest Delights that any rational
Creature can here either expect or
hope for. *Peppa* answer'd not a word
to this Discourse, which *Julia* took as a
good Omen; judging by her silence,
that by little and little she would yield
to Reason: Her Health, which daily
augmented, fortify'd her Opinion, that
the Stranger did not now so much disquiet her.

The Marquess *Spinola* was at *Rome*
when he heard that his Mistress was perfectly recover'd of her Indisposition.
So good News exciting his Passion,
through the Impatience it caus'd in him
of seeing this charming Person, he
thought of nothing but to dispatch his
Voyage to *Genoa*: And having heard
that

that at *Civita Vecchia*, there was a
Squadron of *French* Ships ready to Sail,
which were to put in at *Genoa*, he prefently left *Rome*, in company of two o-
ther Gentlemen of *Genoa*, who were
glad to take the fame opportunity, for
to return to their own Country. They
arriv'd at *Civita Vecchia* the fame day
that the *French* Ships were to depart.
The *Chevalier* of—— that commanded
the whole Squadron, receiv'd them with
a great deal of Civility, taking them
aboard his own Ship. As he had not
been ignorant of the Name, and Quality of the Marquefs *Spinola*, he treated
him with a fingular Refpect. His Table, tho ferv'd with all forts of deli-
cates, was the leaft of the Entertainment. They often drank the health of
Ladies, which oblig'd the Gentlemen
of *Genoa* to tell the *Chevalier*, that the
Marquefs had a Miftrefs, who was certainly the fineft perfon in *Italy*. The
Chevalier infinitely commended the
Beauty of the Ladies in their Country,
and confefs'd, That being at *Genoa* in
the time of the *Carnaval*, he went in
Mafquerade to a Ball, whereof he related to them the particulars; but that
he never was in his life in fo great danger

ger of taking leave of his Liberty, and that he was forc'd to summon all his Reason, to resist a secret inclination for a very amiable person that he had seen at a Ball, whose Name he nevertheless had not enquir'd after. He now thought certainly, that he should never be in love, since that he had escap'd so great a danger. After this Discourse the *Che-valier* drank the Health of the Marquess's Mistress, and to do him the greatest Honour that could be done at Sea, he fir'd all the Guns of his Ship. The Marquess, overjoy'd, told him, That his Mistress was not unworthy of this Honour, and promis'd him, that he should see her as soon as they came to *Genoa*, where they arriv'd soon after.

Peppa was overperswaded by *Julia* to receive favourably the Marquess, altho she design'd to defer her Marriage as long as she could. As soon as the Marquess was arriv'd, he went to wait on the Princess *Doria* his Aunt, who was not a little glad of his return. She carried him into the Appartment of *Peppa*, who answer'd him with expressions more of Compliment than Love, to all the obliging things he said to her. After several Civilities pass'd,
the

the Marquefs let them know the great
obligations he had receiv'd from the
Chevalier of——— when he was aboard
his Ship, with all the marks of Refpects
that he could wifh, fo far as to fire every Gun of his Veffel at the drinking
the Health of the fair *Peppa.* He then
gave them a very advantageous defcription of his Perfon and his good Qualities; and feeing that this recital difpleas'd not the Ladies, he inform'd
them of the Adventure that happen'd to
the *Chevalier* in his Mafquerade, and
how far he forc'd his Inclination to defend himfelf from being in Love with
a lovely Perfon, that he had feen at a
Ball. *Peppa,* who at firft found that the
Defcription of the *Chevalier* was very
like that of her Stranger, remain'd
much difturb'd all the time that the
Marquefs was fpeaking of what had
pafs'd at the Ball, and of all the other
Circumftances which fo exactly refem-
bl'd her Adventure, that the Company
might eafily have perceiv'd the diforder
that fhe was in, if at the fame time, the
Marquefs had not turn'd about to fpeak
to his Aunt in private, for to entreat
her to find fome means to make good
his Promife which he had made to fhew
the

the *Chevalier* his Miſtreſs. The Princeſs, who had a great deal of kindneſs
for her Nephew, took it upon her ſelf
to obtain her Husband's Conſent; and
to accompliſh the better her deſign, ſhe
told the Marqueſs, that ſhe would have
on the morrow, at her Houſe, a Con-
ſort of Muſick with a Collation, to
which ſhe would invite the Ladies of
the Neighbourhood, and that he might
bring with him his Friend. The Marqueſs retir'd well ſatisfy'd with the Expedient that his Aunt had found out,
and did not in the leaſt perceive the
perplexity wherewith the Mind of his
Miſtreſs was agitated. As ſoon as he
was gone, *Peppa* gave an account to her
Couſin of all that ſhe had learnt; and as
her Father had an eſteem always for the
Spaniards, and therefore ſhe being educated all along with Sentiments of Averſi-
for the *French*, ſhe ſhew'd no little
trouble that this Gentleman, whom ſhe
had found ſo agreeable, was a *Frenchman*. *Julia* acquieſc'd in her Opinion, and
added ſeveral ſtrong Arguments to perſwade her from thinking any more of
him. *Peppa* promis'd to follow her
Counſel; but ſhe conjur'd her once more
to lend her Aſſiſtance to find ſome way
whereby

whereby she might see again that dangerous Gentleman, assuring her, that she had no other design, . ' that of discovering, whether this was the Stranger that caus'd all her disquiet. *Julia* full of tenderness for *Peppa*, and altogether as curious, promis'd to contribute her utmost to satisfy her in this point.   They were both busying themselves to find out some means to see this *Chevalier*, without being seen by him, when the Princess *Doria* entring the Chamber where they were, told them, That the next day she would give them a Consort of Musick with a Collation, and that she would invite some Ladies, whom she nam'd to them.   She advis'd them to dress themselves with all the advantage they could , *For may be*, (said she) *the Marquess* Spinola *will bring some* French Gentlemen, *that came from* Rome *with him*.   *Peppa*, o'rejoy'd that Fortune offer'd so happy an opportunity, whereby she might satisfy her Curiosity, spent all the night with much impatience.   She therefore retir'd betimes to her Chamber, and went to bed sooner than her usual hour, as if that would hasten forward the night, and occasion a quicker return of the morning.

ning. Neverthelefs fhe found the time
very long, and was not a little uneafie
in her thoughts. One while fhe pleas'd
her felf to think, that fhe fhould con-
template, at leifure, that dear Object,
which before fhe had feen but a moment,
and which had made fo great an impreffion in her Mind : Then again, fhe
was afraid to fee him, and reprefented
to her felf, a train of inevitable Misfortunes, that would be the Confequence of her refifting the Will of her
Parents. In fpight of all thefe Reflections, the fear of being deceiv'd in her
hopes, caus'd her greateft trouble; for
when fhe began to think that the *Che-*
valier of ——— might not be the Stranger that fhe look'd for, and that all
her affurance for it, was but the Report that fhe had receiv'd of the Adventure of the *Chevalier*, which feem'd to
be like that of her Stranger, fhe therefore would willingly fee him without
running any hazard. In this incerti-
tude, fhe took a great deal of care the
next day to drefs her felf with all the
advantage fhe could, and fhe did not
fail in her defign; for the Princefs *Do-*
ria and *Julia* agreed, that they never
faw her in a Drefs fo magnificent as fhe
was then. The Princefs being perfwa-
                        C   ded,

ded, that she did it to please the Marquess, appear'd extreamly satisfy'd.
It is certain, that the richness of her
Dress gave so much Lustre to her natural Beauty, that all those who saw her,
could not forbear crying out, That
they had never seen so fair a Creature.

The Marquess and the *Chevalier*, accompanied with several of their Friends,
came to the Confort. As soon as they
were enter'd into the Ladies Apartments, *Peppa*, who easily singl'd out the
Chevalier from the rest, was in a great
Confusion. She found, however, such
infinite satisfaction in seeing him again,
that she forgot those Reflections which
she lately made. The Marquess presented his Friend to the Princess *Doria*,
who receiv'd him with much Civility.
They then offer'd their Respects to
Peppa, who had scarce the Courage to
look up. The Marquess transported
with Joy, seeing the great splendour of
her Beauty, could not hold from saying
to the *Chevalier*, That *now he might
judge, whether she did not merit the Honour he did her, when he drank her Health
at the report of all the Guns of his Ship.*
The *Chevalier*, who immediately knew
her to be the same person that appear'd

so

fo beautiful at the Ball two years before,
was in fo great a furprife, and beheld
her fo attentively, that he gave no Anfwer to what the Marquefs faid to him.
This Affection which coft him a great
deal of trouble to overcome the firft
time that he had feen *Peppa*, was now
renew'd ; and he found by fome private motions of his Heart, that it
would be impoffible for him to refift.
Peppa, who fat next to *Julia*, had always her Eyes fix'd on the *Chevalier*:
She found him fo much to her liking,
that far from repenting of thofe amorous Sentiments fhe had for him whilft
he was yet unknown to her; fhe reproach'd her Coufin for her having fo
often blam'd this Amour; and fhe endeavour'd to make her obferve in his
perfon, the new Agreement that fhe
each moment difcover'd. The Marquefs,
who was wholly taken up with the Mu-
fick, liften'd to it with fo much attention, that he did not perceive the Confufion the *Chevalier* was in, and he flatter'd himfelf with the imagination, that
his own prefence might in fome meafure
be the caufe of the Joy which added
fo great a luftre to *Peppa*'s Beauty. As
the *Chevalier* fpoke nothing to him in

praife

praiſe of the Muſick ; he ask'd him if he did not like it ? The *Chevalier* anſwer'd him freely, That *altho he was always a great admirer of Muſick, yet he had not any reliſh for it now, when he had before his Eyes the moſt beautiful perſon of the World.* The Marqueſs perceiving well that *Peppa* had the greateſt ſhare in his Anſwer, aſſur'd his Friend, That the Cuſtom of *Italy* could permit of a familiar Converſation, he would alſo be ſatisfy'd, that her Wit was no ways inferiour to her Beauty. The Collation being ſerv'd up, the Marqueſs pray'd the Princeſs *Doria* to place the *Chevalier* next to *Peppa*, to which the Princeſs eaſily condeſcended, to pleaſe her Nephew. Altho *Peppa* and the *Chevalier* had a ſenſible delight to ſee themſelves ſo near together, yet they were uneaſie in being depriv'd of the pleaſure of beholding one another ; but the *Chevalier* not being willing to loſe ſo happy an opportunity, found means to ſpeak to *Peppa*, without being overheard by any of the Company, That he ſaw it was impoſſible for a perſon to withſtand his Deſtiny; and as for him, he never would complain of his, for he was ſenſible, that he was born to adore her all his life.

The

The Modesty of *Peppa* would not allow
her to give him an Answer to these
Expressions, neverthelesé something in
her Actions let him know, that she was
not displeas'd with what he had said.
The *Chevalier* satisfy'd with the progress
he had made in his Amour, enter'd into
Conversation with the other Ladies,
and took care to say nothing afterwards
but what every one might hear. The
Banquet was concluded with much Magnificence ; altho the *Chevalier* did not
believe it had lasted long enough, yet
before he retir'd, he had the pleasure
to meet the kind looks of his Mistress,
and by this mute Language of their
Eyes, they fully discover'd the Sentiments they had for each other.

The *Chevalier* spent the night without sleeping ; the lovely *Peppa* appearing always in his Thoughts, and he
thought himself the most happy Man in
the World, when that he repass'd over
in his Mind, that she had heard him
without being displeas'd at it, that
even her Eyes had let him understand,
that she had not an indifferent Affection
for him ; but presently making Reflections upon the state of his own Prefer-
ment, foresaw, that being advanc'd in

the

the Service of his King, he could not
receive into his Breaſt ſo great a Paſſion,
and particularly at *Genoa*, without
great hazard of ruining his Fortune.
In ſpight of all theſe Reflections, his
Amour got the Victory of all theſe Com-
motions, and he could not tell which
way to take a Reſolution of parting
from his Miſtreſs. An Order that he
receiv'd upon his Arrival at *Genoa* to
depart immediately for *France*, put him
into the greateſt diſorder imaginable ;
but knowing how nice the King was in
all that related to his Service, he reſolv'd not to admit of the thoughts of
deferring his Voyage one moment, altho he probably believ'd, that he
ſhould never get ſuch another occaſion,
or to agree with her what Methods and
Meaſures to obſerve for the time to
come. In this extremity he reſolv'd to
write to her, for to let her underſtand,
the real motions of his Heart : He deferr'd it not till it was day ; for having
call'd his Servants, he aſk'd for a light,
and writ this following Letter.

*I Once had the thoughts that I ſhould
never be in Love, ſince I had the power to reſiſt its force, when I ſaw you two*
years

years ago. I was confirm'd in this Opinion by infinite Arguments; but I had no sooner seen you a second time, when that all these Arguments, which before had appear'd to me invincible, became weak; and now far from endeavouring to preserve my Liberty, I repent of my former Resistance, and I esteem the time past as lost, not being able to comprehend, that there can be a Felicity in this World, equal to that of loving you. A Duty most cruel, but yet not to be dispens'd with, obliges me to return suddenly into France. *I should have met with a far greater resistance, in resolving this absence, had I not believ'd, that that Man must be unworthy of you, who can fail in his Duty to his King. This reason alone makes me go without hesitating, but with a resolution to make a speedy return, to find you out in what place soever you are ; to adore you continually; and to sacrifice my Life to a Love that is perfect, and constant.*

He found this Letter exactly conformable to his Mind ; but he was in a great perplexity, how to give it to the charming *Peppa,* for he very well knew, that the greatest part of the Nobility of *Genoa* live extreamly retir'd , and

C 4　　　that

that it would be very difficult to have
access into their Houses, and particularly, near their Wives or Daughters. He
fear'd, that if he should commit this Secret to Mercinary Persons, they would
act but faintly in his Affair ; and especially in his absence. He was thus disquie-
ting himself, when that the Count *Centu-*
rione enter'd his Chamber ; he began
to chide him for his unkindness, that he
came not to lodge in his Palace. The
Chevalier excus'd himself upon his short
stay, having an Order to make Sail
from *Genoa* with all expedition. The
Count perceiving him to be very uneasie, conjur'd him to let him know,
whether he could contribute any thing
to his satisfaction; assuring him, that
he would expose both his Life and Fortune in his Service. The *Chevalier,*
sighing, confess'd, That he had plung'd
himself in the most cruel Affair that
he ever met with in all his Life : This
oblig'd the Count to renew the offer
which he had made him before, adding all that he could think of, to perswade him, that he should esteem himself the most happy man in the World,
if he could find an occasion to testify
to him his Acknowledgment. The
Chevalier

Chevalier without any further difficulty, made him a Confident in his Secret. Having in short acquainted him with the beginning of his Adventure, he confess'd, that he was in Love ; and that notwithstanding he could not prevent his departing, and absenting himself from the only person he could love. The Count represented to him, the almost invincible difficulties that he would meet with in his Enterprise ; but however he offer'd him all the Assistance in the World ; and assur'd him, that he would stick at nothing where his Service was in Question. The *Chevalier* shew'd him then the Letter which he had writ, and told him, That he should depart with less trouble, if he would take the charge upon him, to convey it to *Peppa*. The Count ingag'd himself with a great deal of Joy, and promis'd to take such exact Measures, that he might rely upon the safe conveyance of his Letter to his Mistress. They had some other Conversation together before the *Chevalier* embark'd, to whom it was a matter of great Consolation to find a Friend so truly grateful.

Peppa past the night with as little rest as the *Chevalier* : She would some-

times

times ſtart as ſhe began to cloſe her
Eyes, and then would imagin, that all
which had paſs'd the day before, was
but a Dream; but when ſhe recollected
her ſelf, how that ſhe had ſeen diſtinct-
ly the *Chevalier*, and that he had alſo
ſpoke to her in ſuch tender Expreſſions;
ſhe found no little delight in repaſſing
in her Mind, thoſe very words he had
us'd; and baniſh'd all Reflections that
might diminiſh her Joy.   As ſoon as it
was day ſhe went into *Julia*'s Chamber,
whom ſhe awak'd, to talk of her Lover.   She made her take notice how
much Wit was in all his Diſcourſe, and
even applauded his Diſcretion, for his
having ſpoke ſo little to her in private.
Julia, either to do Juſtice to the *Chevalier*, or out of Complaiſance for her
Couſin, own'd, that if a weakneſs of this
nature might be pardonable in a young
Maid, ſhe was far leſs criminal than
another, ſince the *Chevalier* in all his
Actions appear'd ſo graceful,   After a
long Diſcourſe, *Peppa*, who flatter'd
her ſelf, that Love might ſtill procure
ſome new means for her to ſee him a-
gain, took no little care in adorning
her ſelf.   She was all the day long
mightily diſcompos'd, and, under
                                          ſome

some pretext or other, visited the Balconies, and all the Windows of the Palace *Doria*. She was in this diligent search, when she heard the sound of several great Guns, which mov'd her Curiosity to enquire into the Reasons: And being told, that the Gallies of the Republick saluted the *French* Ships which were under Sail. This news much surpris'd her, because she could not have imagin'd, that the *Chevalier*, after the declaring himself to her as he had done, was capable of departing, without letting her hear from him. She was sensibly touch'd with this appearance of Contempt, and call'd to her Remembrance all that she had heard reported to the disadvantage of the *French* Nation, who had this general Character in their Neighbouring Countries, that they could easily ingage themselves in any Amour, and as easily quit it again, without the least concern in the World. She bemoan'd her misfortune to *Julia*, and in the angry humour she was in, endeavouring to lessen all that was charming in the *Chevalier*, she promis'd her never to think more of this Ingrate.

We must now leave the *Chevalier* pursuing

purſuing his Voyage to *France* in a ſtormy ſeaſon of the year, and upon an unruly Sea ; but whether that or his Paſſion was his greateſt care, this Song, the product of his ſolitary Thoughts, will beſt teſtifie. He ſent it with the firſt Ship, for his Friend *Centurione* at *Genoa*, who till a long time after, could·not meet with an opportunity of putting it into the Hands of the fair *Peppa*.

OH my Zelinda ! could you

ſee the fury of each foaming Wave,

you'd think, that the tempeſtuous Sea

would

would e'ry moment be our Grave:

But, oh Zelinda! could you view

the greater Tempest in my Heart,

you'd know that it was rais'd for you;

So sad, so sad 'tis to depart; so

sad, so sad 'tis to depart.

2.

Come to my aid some gentle Wind,
　And thus my Am'rous Message bear ;
Tell all the troubles of my Mind,
　And whisper how I love my Fair :
Tell her my Fancy all the day
　Doth still enjoy her glorious sight ;
But tell her too, that absence may
　Involve me in eternal Night.
　　Involve me, &c.

The

The Affembly of the Relations of both Families, which fhould have met long before, upon the treaty of Marriage between the Marquefs *Spinola* and *Peppa*, but which was then deferr'd by reafon of *Peppa's* illnefs, met two days after the *Chevalier* fet Sail. They regulated the Affairs on each fide, and refolv'd to have them married immediately. *Peppa*, who could not forget the *Chevalier*, in fpight of all his Ingratitude, being inform'd of this Refolution, went prefently into the Chamber of her Coufin, where fhe gave her felf wholly up to her Grief and Tears, without having the pow'r to utter one word. *Julia* did what fhe could to comfort her, and advis'd her to obey willingly her Parents, and not to hazard the Content of her whole life, by a vexatious oppofition. She added, *That it was part of her good Fortune to be undeceiv'd of the* Chevalier, *fince fhe had now found by her own Experience, that he never had a true kindnefs for her. I believe all that you fay*, interrupted *Peppa*, *but yet you muft acknowledge, that I am the moft unhappy perfon that breaths, feeing that I am going to be facrifis'd to a Man that I can never love, when he a-*
lone,

*lone, whom I thought worthy of my Love,
shuns me.* The many fighs and tears,
which ftifled her Voice, hinder'd her
from proceeding any further in her
Complaints.

In the mean while that *Julia*, who
fhar'd in her Coufins forrow, lamented
with her, the Count *Centurione*, who
was to convey to *Peppa* the Letter given by the *Chevalier*, try'd all manner
of ways to gain one of the Women
that waited on her. After feveral Intreagues, finding that his endeavours
to win her to him prov'd fruitlefs,he told
her at laft, as a fecret, that fhe might
deliver it without the leaft apprehenfi-
ons, fince that this Letter came from
the Marquefs *Spinola*, who did only defign to furprize his Miftrefs, and to fee
if fhe could guefs whence it came. The
Servant being overperfwaded by this
falfe appearance, took charge of the
Letter, and prefented it to her Lady.
Peppa fomething amaz'd at this novelty,
demanded from whom fhe receiv'd it.
The Servant anfwer'd her, That fhe
was forbid to tell, but that fhe would
foon know in reading it. *Peppa*, who
at firft confulted only her Honour, refus'd to receive it, but as foon as fhe
was

was alone, she repented that she had
let it go, imagining, that it might have
come from the *Chevalier.* A hundred
times was she going to have ask'd her
Servant for it, and as many times her
Modesty and her Fear, that it was the
Marquess *Spinola* who had sent it, hinder'd her. In fine, after several Irre-
folutions, her Curiosity, or rather, her
Love, got the victory. She sent after
the Servant, and threaten'd to turn her
away, unless she would declare from
whence the Letter came. The Servant,
still reserving that as a Mystery, deliver'd it without making her any Answer. *Peppa,* for all her Modesty, had not
the power to resist her Curiosity to
know what was in it ; she read the Letter, and immediately retir'd in private, to abandon her self without any
constraint, to all the transport of Joy
that this pleasant perusal had caus'd in
her. She read it a thousand times, and
a thousand times she repented of the
disadvantageous Opinion that she had
had of her Lover. Her Marriage,
which was brought now to a conclusion,
was a trouble to her not to be imagin'd.
Her Love, notwithstanding, gave her still
some hopes to find out a Pretext to defer

fer this Marriage: She refolv'd, even
at laft, to feign her felf fick, and to
make ufe of all her Addrefs, to prevent
this Affair from being concluded. In
the mean time fhe bufied her Thoughts
for an Anfwer to the *Chevalier*; which
near upon was exprefs'd in thefe words.

*THE Rules of Modefty would fcarce
permit me to anfwer a Letter that
was fo full of Gallantries as yours, but
the fame Deftiny which has ingag'd you in
an efteem for me, does likewife compel me
to do that for you alone, which I thought
never to have done for any. I would
therefore have you believe, That your
Cares for me will not be unwelcome, and
that I fhall receive no fmall delight when
I may fee you again.*

Peppa, fuppofing that the *Chevalier*
had found the fafeft way to hear from
her, was content to take no further
care, but only to remit this Anfwer into the Hands of the Servant who gave
her the Letter, not doubting but that fhe
would be faithful in the delivery; her
Modefty not permitting her to enquire
into the meafures that were to be taken.
This Maid being prepoffefs'd, that the
                                        Count

Count *Centarione* was of the Plot with
the Marquefs *Spinola*, and that the Anfwer which her Miftrefs gave her was
really for the Marquefs, met him by
chance a moment after: She was fo
pleas'd with her Negotiation, that it
was impoffible for her to hide her Joy.
You fave me the trouble to go any further,
faid fhe to him, in giving him the Letter from *Peppa*. She withdrew without
ftaying for his Anfwer, for fear that fhe
fhould be feen to talk with him. The
Marquefs, who knew the Hand of his
Miftrefs, tafted before-hand all the
Pleafure that a paffionate Lover can conceive in having a Letter deliver'd to him
from a perfon whom he entirely loves;
but after that he had perceiv'd in
reading it, that it was defign'd for another, and not for him, he was feiz'd
with Horrour and Amazement, never
having had the leaft thoughts that *Peppa*
was capable of a Love Entreague: His
Indignation and Anger gave him not
leifure to make any further Reflections;
he enter'd the Chamber of the Princefs
Doria full of grief, and giving her the
Letter, utter'd a thoufand Reproaches;
that fhe would have had him marry'd a
perfon who was fo falfe to him. The
Princefs

Princefs furpris'd at this fury of her
Nephew, and the Expreffions fo little
refpectful which he us'd, read the Letter which he gave her. She ask'd then
the Marquefs, to whom this Letter was
directed, and by what adventure it fell
into his Hands. *I cannot fatisfy you in
that*, anfwer'd the Marquefs, *I know
very well that Peppa preferves all her
Love for another, whilft that I am going
to marry her. It was one of her Women
that gave me this Letter; you fee hereby
that fhe was miftaken, and it muft be
without doubt that fhe was not well in-
ftructed.* The Princefs made the Woman be call'd, whom the Marquefs had
nam'd, and after having told her, that
fhe fhould undergo the fevereft effects
of her Anger, if fhe did not declare
the truth; fhe aks'd her the meaning
of this Letter. The Woman confefs'd,
That the Count *Centurione* had given her
one to deliver to *Peppa*, that fhe had
acquitted her felf of the charge laid upon her, and had got an Anfwer, which
fhe put into the Hands of the Marquefs
Spinola, believing, as the Count *Centurione* had affur'd her, That they were
both of Council together, and that it
was all one to deliver the Letter to
either

either of them, since that the Count
had no other design, but what was only
for the Interest of the Marquess. This
Answer made them believe, that the
Woman had been deceiv'd. The
Princess conjur'd her Nephew to have a
little Patience, and to let her have
time to search into the bottom of this
Intreague, assuring him, that she would
be the first that would break off his
Marriage, if she found that *Peppa* held
the least Correspondance with the
Count *Centurione*. The Marquess dis-
sembled, as well as he could, his Despair, promising, that he would patiently expect the event, and so retir'd.
The Princess without losing one moment of time, secur'd first the Servant,
shutting her up in a Chamber, whereof
she her self kept the Key. She pass'd
from thence into the Apartment of
her Daughter-in-law, and told her as
soon as she came in, That she would ac-
quaint her with such News which would
surprize her. *Peppa* was impatient till
she knew it. *We have discover'd,* continu'd the Princess, *that the Marquess*
Spinola *is so strictly ingag'd with a Lady*
of Rome, *that it is not in his power to*
marry any other, which makes your Father
                                    resolve

refolve to hearken to the *Count* Centurione, *who earnestly demands you in Marriage: He gave me a charge that I should
make you acquainted with his defign,* and
*to prepare you to receive kindly this new
Lover, whom he himfelf will offer to you
to morrow.* Peppa was wholly furpriz'd
at this Difcourfe which fhe fo little
expected. She conjur'd her Mother-in-
law, with tears in her Eyes, to hinder
the effects of fo fudden a Refolution,
telling her, That fhe could not take up
a Refolution of marrying a Man whom
fhe had never feen, and hardly knew
his Name. *However*, anfwer'd the
Princefs, *your Father did not determine
this Affair, but upon the confideration that
he was affur'd you have a great kindnefs
for this Count.* Peppa protefted to her
over again, That fhe did not know
him, and declar'd, that fhe had rather live all her days in a Nunnery,
than to confent to fuch a Marriage. *I
have never heard,* anfwer'd the Princefs,
*in a ferious tone, that when one writes
kind Letters to any perfon, they do not at
the fame time know who they are.* Peppa
touch'd with thefe laft words, anfwer'd
her coldly, That fhe knew not what
fhe meant; and that without doubt
                                        fome

fome perfon, envious of her happinefs,
made ufe of this Contrivance to ruin
her in the Opinion of all her Friends.
The Princefs faid, She was forry that
fhe muft be forc'd to convince her;
and to let her fee that fhe had invented
nothing of her own Head, told her,
That fhe need only follow her; fhe
brought her to the Chamber wherein
fhe had fhut the Maid, whom fhe call'd
by her Name, as foon as fhe had open'd
the Door; but was mightily furpriz'd
to find no body. This Maid frighten'd by the threatnings of the Princefs, had found means to efcape out
by a private Door that was behind the
Hangings, and fhe left *Genoa* with fo
much Diligence and Caution, that it was
impoffible for the Princefs to difcover,
whither fhe was gone. *Peppa*, who
was really innocent of any Intreague
with the Count, but yet had fear'd the
difcovery of her Affair with the *Chevalier*, from the mouth of this Servant,
became now more bold, by the abfence
of the only perfon that could confront
her, and reproach'd the Princefs for
her Injuftice, in fufpecting her fo light-
ly. The Printefs touch'd with the Reproaches of her Daughter-in-law,
hop'd

hop'd ftill to convince her by the Letter that was in the Hands of the Marquefs, to whom fhe writ, for to pray him to fend it her; but it was in vain, for the Marquefs, not being capable of receiving Comfort for the Infidelity of his Miftrefs, nor of pardoning the Count *Centurione* the Artifice that he us'd to make the Servant take charge of his Letter, refolv'd to fight him; and having met him by chance the fame day, he made him draw, after having torn in his prefence, *Peppa*'s Letter, although the Count declar'd, that he was not his Rival, and that this Letter was not directed to him. They fought fome time with an almoft equal advantage; but in fine, Fortune declar'd for *Centurione*, and *Spinola* was worfted. This Affair made great noife at *Genoa*; there was fcarce a perfon but what talk'd of it, and ftrove to fearch into the Subject of their Quarrel. Thefe two Gentlemen, had neverthelefs fo much Difcretion, that no body could difcover, that the Daughter of the Prince *Doria* had any fhare in the Action. The Princefs inform'd of the Misfortune of her Nephew, and of the Declaration which *Centurione* had made to him before

fore he would draw his Sword, began to
believe that there was some Myſtery
hid in this Affair, and that may be ſome
perſon, who envy'd the Grandeur of
the two Families, had us'd this perfidious ſtratagem to breed a Diſturbance,
when they oblig'd the Servant to deliver the Marqueſs this Letter of *Peppa's*, whoſe Hand without doubt they
had counterfeited. All the circumſtances of this Intrigue, and particularly, the flight of this Servant, confirm'd her in theſe thoughts; and as
one is apt to believe thoſe things which
one wiſhes, ſhe reſted ſatisfy'd, that
Peppa had been betray'd, and was reconcil'd to her. The Princeſs was then
willing to undeceive the Marqueſs; but
whether that he was not ſo eaſie to be
perſwaded as his Aunt, or that he was
aſham'd of the advantage that *Centurione* had had over him, he went from
Genoa without taking leave of any one,
and paſs'd into the Emperours Army,
which was then in it's March to raiſe the
Siege of *Vienna*.

The ſudden abſence of the Marqueſs
Spinola ſurpris'd every body, and much
troubl'd the Princeſs *Doria*, who hereby ſaw all her hopes fruſtrated, and the

D   Union

Union of the two Families as far off as
ever. Her Husband himself was much
offended at so extravagant a way of
acting, and began to hearken favourably to the Proposals that one of his
Friends made to him, which was to give
his Daughter to the Marquess of *Villa
Mediana Celi*, first Minister of *Spain*,
and who serv'd at *Milan*, at the Head
of a Regiment of Foot. He gave him
for example, the Marquess of *Los Bal-
baxes*, who went for one of the most
cunning Polititians that had been in *Genoa* of a long time, who was more af-
sur'd of the Protection of *Spain*, by
marrying his Children to the *Spaniards*,
than by his long Services. The Prince
Doria was mov'd by these reasons, and
promis'd his Friend to consider seriously
of it. The Marquess of *Villa Mediana*
having had notice of the favourable Inclination that the Prince *Doria* had for
him, and finding that *Peppa* was one of
the richest Heiresses of *Italy*, came to
Genoa in all diligence. The Prince *Doria* receiv'd him very civilly ; which ingag'd him to make use of all the Gallantries which were practis'd in *Spain*. He
walk'd the greatest part of the night
under *Peppa's* Window, and in the day
never

never fail'd to be at all the Churches
that she usually went to ; but *Peppa*,
who still flatter'd her self with the
thoughts of seeing quickly again the
Chevalier, had the malice never to regard this diligence of the *Spaniard*, who
neverthelefs did not difpair, but hop'd
that in the end his Conſtancy would
prevail. In all his Serenades, Songs
were not wanting , that declar'd the
ſtrength of a Paſſion ; like this that follows.

Lovely Cœlia, let your Ear

liſten to my humble Pray'r ; let it

hear your dying Lover ; let it hear,

and

and then discover how innocent,

and free I am from flattery.   How

little all! How little all the World

I prize, to one kind glance from

Cœlia's

Cœlia's Eyes! To one kind glance

from Cœlia's Eyes.

2.

Welcome Shores to those that are
Shipwrack'd, and of Life despair,
Or t'Offenders Pardon given.
Or to th'Holy Man his Heaven,
   Not greater Pleasures be,
   Than Cœlia kind to me.
So little all the World I prize,
To one kind glance from Cœlia's Eyes.

In the mean while that he forgot nothing that would produce fuccefs, the
Marchionefs *Durazzo* took her Daughter home, for to put her afterwards into the Nunnery, whereto fhe was defign'd. *Peppa*, who had never hid any
thing from her Coufin, and who found
a great deal of Comfort in difclofing
her Thoughts to her without any conftraint, was fo afflicted at this parting,
that fhe begg'd her Parents to let her
be enter'd fome time into the Nunnery
where *Julia* went to take the Veil;
but her Father would never confent to
it, which oblig'd her to lead a life very retir'd, fcarce going out of her
Chamber, and without any other Pleafure but what the hopes gave her of the
return of her Lover. The Count *Centurione* had not fail'd to write to *France*,
and to inform him of the Deftiny of
his Letter, and of all that had pafs'd at
Genoa, fince he was gone; and even
gave him hopes, that if he would fend
another Letter, he would leave nothing
untry'd that might procure him an Anfwer. The *Chevalier* fent him a fecond
Letter, full of paffionate expreffions,
which fet his Thoughts on work, how
to

to deliver it. The Zeal that he had for the Service of his Friend, ingag'd him to write with the most certain promises, that he would procure him greater success in the delivery of this second Letter, than there was in that of the first. However, as he knew no body that had access near *Peppa*, and she leading a life very retir'd, since her Cousin was not with her, it was impossible for *Centurione* to convey his Friend's Letter to her. He inform'd himself of all those who had acquaintance in the Palace *Doria*, if *Peppa* had not some particular Friends, whom she lov'd to converse with; he understood that she lov'd *Julia* very well, and that she would admit of no Comfort for her Absence. The Count despairing of doing any thing for his Friend, reproach'd himself every moment with his want of Industry, was afraid, that the *Chevalier*, who had trusted him with an Affair so delicate, might either have some belief that he kept Intelligence with his Rival; or, that he acted but weakly for his Interest, since that he acquitted himself no better in the charge he had undertaken, after he having en-

D 4　　gag'd

gag'd himſelf in the attempt, and promis'd even a fortunate ſucceſs.   The
remembrance of the great Obligations
that he hath receiv'd from the *Chevalier*, and the generous means that he
us'd in his Affair; this put him quite
into deſpair.   But when that he con-
ſider'd, that the *Chevalier* might with
the ſooneſt opportunity arrive at *Genoa*, and come ſecretly to his Houſe,
in hopes to hear ſome good news, and
yet he had nothing to tell him: This
laſt thought put him into ſo great a
confuſion, that he could with Pleaſure
have quitted the beſt part of his Eſtate,
to find an occaſion of being ſerviceable
to his Friend, and to give him a teſti-
mony of his Acknowledgment.   In this
extremity, he took ſo extraordinary a
Reſolution, that no example of Friend-
ſhip can parallel.   He had a particular
acquaintance with the Marqueſs *Durazzo*, who was one of the chief Senators
of *Genoa*.   He one day made him a Viſit, and after having declar'd to him in
obliging expreſſions, the eſteem that he
had for his perſon, he told him, That
he ſhould be very glad to enter into
the Alliance of a Man of his worth, and
to

to become his Son-in-law. The Marquefs, who knew very well the great Eftate of *Centurione*, anfwer'd him, fmiling, That his Daughters were not Fortunes for him, nor had that vanity to think of fuch a Perfon as he was, who could make Pretenfions to any of the richeft Fortunes of the City. *Centurione* reply'd, That he was not of the humour of the other *Genoefes*, who in fetling themfelves, minded lefs the fatisfaction of their Minds, than procuring vaft Eftates; but that for him, he fhould think himfelf extreamly happy in marrying one his Daughters; affuring him, that no manner of Articles between them fhould break off the Match. The Marquefs charm'd with this noble Action of *Centurione*, told him, That two of his Daughter were already Nuns, that he had two others remaining at home, one whereof was brought up with the Daughter of the Prince *Doria*, and juft upon taking the Veil; That if he perfifted in the fame Sentiments he already had declar'd, he might confult with his Friends about it, and returning to him again, fhould then be able to give him a pofitive Anfwer. The Count retir'd

D 5   very

very well satisfy'd ; and as he was long
before capable of governing himself and
his Estate, it was not difficult for him to
obtain the consent of his Relations. The
Marquess on his side, consulted his
Friends : His Wife, who perceiv'd that
Julia had no great Inclination for the
Cloister, was overjoy'd at the Proposition of Count *Centurione* : She was very scrupulous of putting her Daughter
into a Nunnery against her Will, which
made her perswade her Husband to let
her want no advantage, rather than
lose a Match so important. The Count
Centurione, who in marrying *Julia*, was
sure of easily seeing *Peppa*, and of ad-
vancing towards this fair person, the
Pretensions of his Friend, return'd to
the House of the Marquess *Durazzo*,
and was receiv'd very favourably both
by the Husband and Wife. The Affair
being concluded the same day, the Marquess presented *Centurione* to his Daughter, and exhorted her in his presence,
to acknowledge all her life time, how
much she was oblig'd to the Count, who
preferr'd her with a small Fortune, before divers Matches that would have
been to him very advantageous. *Julia*,
to. whom such a happiness came unexpected,

pested, especially in a Country where
the Estate regulates the Marriages, receiv'd the Count with all the Marks
of Esteem, and acknowledgement that
he could wish, and they were married
a little while after with an equal satisfaction on both sides. *Peppa* was at
all the Ceremonies, and was so joyful
for her Cousin's good Fortune, that she
gave infinite Praises to the Count, for
the Generosity that he shew'd. The
Princess *Doria* who then thought she
saw further into this Business than the
others, rested satisfied that the Count
had been of a long time in Love with
Julia, and that the Letter which had
caus'd so much Trouble to her Nephew,
was the hand of this Kinswoman, who
writ much like *Peppa*, because they had
learnt of the same Master.

The Count who saw *Peppa* every day,
finding himself capable of serving his
Friend, prepar'd a great Feast in his
Palace, and did resolve to take hold
of this Opportunity for to speak to
this lovely Person in behalf of the Chevalier, delivering into her hands the
Letter whereof he had took Charge.
And as he was infinitely contented with
his Wife, and not enduring to hide any
thing

thing from her, he confefs'd to her
one day, after having affur'd her of his
conftant Love, that he efteem'd himfelf the happieft Man alive, in having
married her ; but that neverthelefs he
was beholden to one of his Friends for
this great happinefs, who had rendred
him the higheft Obligation that ever
Man receiv'd. He then told her, that
this Friend was in Love with *Peppa*,
and that he had ingag'd himfelf to fpeak
to her in his behalf ; but that he refolv'd
not to attempt it without asking her
Advice. *Julia* furpris'd at her Husband's
Difcourfe, counfel'd him forthwith, to
undeceive his Friend, and told as a
fecret, that her Coufin was already fo
taken with a ftranger, that tho' fhe had
made ufe of all her Intereft to exclude
his Memory from her Thoughts, fhe
found it was but to little purpofe, and
that her Coufin was refolv'd never to
forget him. *You did then oppofe the Intereft of my Friend*, interrupted the
Count ? *I doubt very much*, replyed Julia, *whether you know him that I mean.*
The *Count* was going to give her an
Anfwer, when he was inform'd that
two ftrangers very earneftly inquir'd
for him. He went out to know what
they

they desir'd of him, and was sometime
without knowing who they were. He
perceiv'd at laft, that he whom he
fpoke to was the *Chevalier*————who
was come to *Genoa* privately in a Dif-
guife, and accompanied only with one
Servant. The *Count* was overjoy'd to
fee him, and carried him into a ftate-
ly Appartment, that he had already
prepar'd for him, and where the *Chevalier* chang'd his Habit for that which
was more fuitable to his Quality. They
had together a long Difcourfe. *Centurione* gave him an Account of all that
had paft at *Genoa* fince his Abfence, and
particularly of the Motifs of his Marriage. The *Chevalier* confounded with
thefe extraordinary Obligations which
he had receiv'd from his Friend, could
not find words capable of expreffing
how fenfible he was of fo true a Friend-
fhip. The *Count* told him that this very day there was to be in his Palace
a great Feaft, the Order whereof the
Princefs *Doria* had taken upon her felf
to regulate, and gave him alfo to
underftand, that perhaps he might procure him the Converfation of his Miftrefs; but becaufe he had need of his
Wifes help to fucceed, he refolv'd to
introduce

introduce the *Chevalier* into her Prefence firſt, and thereupon he enter'd
his Wifes Chamber, to prepare her
for this Viſit. He inform'd her of the
Arrival of his Friend; and after having exaggerated to her the important
fervice that this Friend had render'd
him, he prayed her to receive him
with all imaginable kindneſs for his
fake. *Julia* who defir'd nothing fo
much as to pleaſe her Husband, promis'd him to follow his Orders, but
ſhe aſſur'd him again, that the greateſt
piece of Service, and of moſt Advantage for his Friend, would be to counfel him to think no more of her Coufin. *Let not that trouble you,* anſwered
the *Count, may be that* Peppa *is not of
your Mind.* He went out without ſtaying for her Anſwer, return'd a moment after, accompanied with the *Chevalier.* *Julia,* who knew him at firſt
fight, to be her Coufin's Lover, was
in fo great a furprize, that ſhe could
fcarce return the Civilities of the *Chevalier;* and complaining to her Husband,
that he did not reveal to her his Friend's
Name. *Judge you,* anſwered the *Count,
whether I had beſt counfel him to think no
more of your Coufin?* A Colour that
over-

overfpread *Julia*'s Face, hinder'd her
from replying. The reft of their Difcourfe was of the Feaft ; They found
it neceffary that the *Chevalier* fhould
not appear; but that he fhould remain
hid in the *Count*'s Appartment.

The Princefs *Doria* and *Peppa* arriv'd
fome time after at the Count *Centurie-
one*'s Palace. The Feaft was carried on
with a great deal of Magnificence ; and
the Marquefs of *Villa Mediana*, who
would not lofe any Opportunity to be
at all the Places where he might fee
Peppa, appear'd in a Mask followed by
feveral Slaves, wearing about their
Necks Collars, with a Motto in Spanifh, which fignifies in our Lauguage,
Our Mafter has no more Liberty than we ;
but he was fo little difguis'd, that
every one knew who he was. *Peppa*,
who could no longer fuffer the tirefome
Gallantries of this Marquefs, drew near
to her Coufin, and told her, that fhe
had refolv'd to come no more to thefe
kind of Feafts, that fhe might be deliver'd from the Importunities of this
Spaniard, who indeavour'd to infufe
Love into her Breaft at a Time when
fhe had fo much Reafon to be afflicted,
being feparated from her Lover, and
ftill

ftill in an uncertainty of feeing him a-
gain. *Julia* promis'd her with an Accent which fhew'd the Aftonifhment fhe
was in at a Paffion fo conftant, that
if the Picture of the *Chevalier* could
give her any Confolation, fhe would
fhew her one in her Husband's Clofet,
which reprefented him fo lively, that
fhe would be furpris'd at it. *Peppa*,
whofe Curiofity was very great in any
Thing that related to her Amour, conjur'd her Coufin not to defer the giving
her this Satisfaction, and of conduct-
ing her to this Clofet. They wanted
not a pretence to get out from the
Company, and went directly to the
Count's Clofet, where he was alone
with the *Chevalier*. Never was any Surprize more pleafing than *Peppa*'s, when
fhe beheld her Lover. The *Chevalier*
caft himfelf at her Feet, and affur'd
her, that he would now forget his
paft Misfortune, fince he enjoy'd the
pleafure of feeing the Perfon that in
the World was moft dear to him. *Peppa*,
who was unprepar'd for a happinefs
fo extraordinary, was at firft in fome
Confufion that her Lover fhould exprefs himfelf fo paffionately in the
Prefence of *Centurione*; and feeking
to

to fave her Honour, which she imagin'd this Interview might blemish,
she complain'd to her Coufin of the
Cheat she had impos'd on her. *Julia*
prefently gueffing the Caufe of her
Confufion, told her that her Husband
was infinitely oblig'd to the *Chevalier*,
that they hid nothing from one another, and that she might declare her
privateft Thoughts before him without
any Referve. *Peppa* taking Courage at
this Difcourfe of her Coufin, did no
longer diffemble the Joy that she had
of feeing the *Chevalier*. They difcover'd to each other all that had paffed,
and gave an interchangeable Account
of all the difturbances they had under-
gone fince they had feen one another.
Their Converfation had lafted much
longer, if *Julia*, who fearing that the
Princefs *Doria* would be in fearch for
her Daughter, had not advis'd her to
make hafte to return, for fear that she
deferr'd it too long, she might be fent
for, whereby that which they defign'd
to keep fecret, would be difcover'd.
Peppa being afraid left her Mother
should find her in this place, prepar'd
to follow her Coufin's Advice, but she
made fo little hafte, that *Julia* was for-
ced

ced to take her by the hand, and carry
her away almoſt by force. The Count
feeing that the *Chevalier*, being depriv'd
of what he lov'd, was in a condition
which caus'd Pity, engag'd his Wife
to make an Invitation for the next day,
and directed her chiefly to get a Promiſe from the Princeſs *Doria*, that ſhe
would bring *Peppa* with her again. The
hopes of feeing one another the next
day, diminiſh'd the Sore that the two
Lovers had to be ſeparated; and
Julia acquitted her ſelf ſo well of the
Commiſſion that her Husband gave her,
that the Princeſs promis'd to leave her
Daughter with her on the morrow all
the day long. *Peppa* appear'd to be in
a very good Humour during the Remainder of the Feaſt. The Marqueſs
of *Villa Mediana*, who expounded every thing to his Advantage, flatter'd
himſelf that his Cares did not diſpleaſe
her; and as he had never ſeen her ſo
Handſome as ſhe was that day, he all
along beheld her with a particular Attention. *Peppa* laugh'd to her ſelf at
the vain Cares of the Marqueſs, and
was ſometimes ſo malicious as to caſt a
Look towards him, but after ſuch a
manner as ſhould not give him cauſe to
have

have the least Hope; however a *Spaniard* flatters himself much more then another Man, and particularly in Love. The Marquess of *Villa Mediana* imagin'd that he was no longer indifferent to *Peppa*. Upon this ground he writ to the *Spanish* Court, and let his Relations understand that he had the esteem of *Peppa*, and that if the King of *Spain* would take notice of it to the Prince *Doria*, his Marriage would infallibly be accomplish'd.

In the mean while the Countess *Centurione* fail'd not to go the next day to the Palace *Doria*, for to desire the Princess to keep the Promise which she had made her. The Princess who was now very well satisfied with her Daughter's Conduct, and who endeavour'd to put out of her mind by all sorts of Complaisance, the injustice that she believ'd to have done her in suspecting her of a Love-Intrigue, consented without any difficulty, that the two Cousins should go out together, and promis'd within a little while to come to them. The *Chevalier* who expected his Mistress with the highest impatience, was in extraordinary transports of Joy at her coming; and whether the

care

care fhe had taken in her Drefs, or the
Pleafure in beholding whom fhe lov'd,
gave a new Luftre to her Beauty, he
fancy'd, that he had never feen her fo
handfome before.

Although their Difcourfe was held
in the Prefence of the Count *Centurione*
and his Wife, it was notwithftanding
intirely moving and paffionate; and
as the Bufinefs of the State did touch
both their particular Intereft, they alfo
fpoke of that. *Peppa* acknowledg'd to
the *Chevalier*, that it was a trouble to
her, to behold the Conduct of thofe
that govern'd the Republick, who
took no care to put a ftop to the
Complaints that the King of *France*
had made againft them, whereof fhe
fear'd the Confequence for the Intereft
of her Family, and for the further Obftacle that it might occafion to her
own happinefs. The *Chavalier* affur'd
her, that whilft he was affur'd of her
Love, the differences between the King
and the Republick fhould never.give
him any Trouble, fince that there was
not any probability that fo many great
Men, which, as he had heard, did com-
pofe the Senate of *Genoa*, could think
to refift a Monarch who had compell'd
fome

some of the greatest Powers of *Europe* to accept the Conditions of Peace that he had offer'd them. *Peppa*, and *Centurione* approv'd of those Reasons, and the *Chevalier* added, that after all these beginnings of diforder were over, he flatter'd himself with the hopes that His Majesty would give him leave to return to *Genoa*, and to demand *Peppa* publickly of her Relations. This lovely Perfon figh'd at his Propofal, and as she knew that the *Chevalier* expos'd himself to all forts of dangers, she conjur'd him to fpare himself a little for her fake, and to think how that she should never be comforted for his Lofs, and that therefore he ought to endeavour something in the Favour of a Perfon whofe Life was wound up in his Deftiny. So much goodnefs piercing the very Soul of the *Chevalier*, made him vow to her, that he was in difpair to think of parting; but neverthelefs his Honour, his Duty, and the attendance that he ow'd to the King his Mafter, oblig'd him to depart inftantly for *Toulon*, there to receive the neceffary Orders from Court. *Peppa* did not difapprove of his Reafons; she prayed him only that he would take all Opportunities to write to her, and

bid

bid him remember that this would be
the only Pleasure she should receive in
his Absence. She could not utter these
last words without melting into Tears,
which so sensibly touch'd the *Chevalier*,
that he was ready to dye with Grief
at the feet of his Charming Mistress.
The Count and his Wife took care to
separate them before the Princess came,
and were forc'd to deceive them both,
for to prevent their Sorrow in taking
leave of one another. They told the
Chevalier that his Mistress was return'd
to her Father's, and assur'd *Peppa* that
her Lover went away, that he might
not be the cause of her relapsing into
the like passionate Tenderness. And
indeed he departed with his Friend,
and return'd with the greatest speed
possible into *France*.

Peppa remain'd so full of Grief for
the departure of her Lover, that without listning to the Reasons that her
Cousin alledg'd, to oblige her to overcome the disorder she was in, for fear
lest the Princess *Doria* should surprize
her in this Condition, she abandon'd
he self to her Grief, and was in Tears
at the very moment that the Princess
came. The Countess at first was in
great

great confusion, both for her Cousin
and her self; but she supplied by the
readiness of her Wit, the Indiscretion
of *Peppa*, for it coming into her mind
to hide a little Dog, that her Cousin
lov'd very well, she went to receive
the Princess in an Anti-Chamber, and
told her that he came in a good time
to comfort *Peppa*, who was in the utmost affliction, because she had lost her
Dog. The Princess finding her Daughter in Tears, told her that her Age
did not admit of so much grief for the
loss of a Dog, and that it would not
be difficult to procure another as handsome as that which occasion'd those
Tears. The Countess assur'd her, that
she would ingage for the finding him
again, but *Peppa* appear'd not the less
afflicted, and went away a little while
after with the Princess *Doria*. However foreseeing that her Cousin might
perhaps send her Dog the next day,
she privately pray'd her before she
went out, to keep him at least a
Week, that the pretence of her Sorrow might remain, lest otherwise
the Truth might be suspected.

The Princess *Doria*, who had sent a
Man that she could trust into *Germany*,

for

for to inform her Nephew of the Count
Centurione's Marriage, and for to clear
all the doubts which might have still remain'd in his Mind, receiv'd, about the
same time, a very obliging Letter from
the Marquess, which return'd thanks
for her kindness, and exprefs'd to her
the great forrow that afflicted him for
having difpleas'd *Peppa*; he intreated
further his Aunt to fpeak in his Favour,
and that he would expect an Anfwer at
Venice, affuring her, that he would not
go from thence till his Mistress had
pardon'd him. The Princess, who
cunningly manag'd this Affair, waited
for a favourable opportunity to shew
her Daughter-in-law her Nephew's Letter. In the mean time *Don Carlos Ba-
can*, Envoy from *Spain* to the Republick
of *Genoa*, went to the Prince *Doria*, as
from the King his Mafter, to intimate
to him, that this Monarch declar'd himfelf for the Intereft of the Marquess
of *Villa Mediana*; and that he could not
by a more fenfible mark, demonftrate
his good Affection towards the Court of
Spain, than by receiving this Gentleman for his Son-in-law; affuring him,
that in favour of this Marriage, he
would give him, when Opportunities
did

did occur, all the marks of Efteem that he could defire. The Prince *Doria* receiv'd, with a profound Refpect, the Honour that the King of *Spain* did him, and affur'd *Don Carlos Bafan*, that he would immediately advife with his Family about it; and that he would ever obferve that Submiffion which was due to the Command of fo great a Monarch. The Princefs *Doria* was very much alarm'd at this Negotiation; notwithftanding fhe manag'd her Husband's Mind with fo much Addrefs, and gave him fuch good Reafons, to let him fee that the Marriage with the Marquefs *Spinola* was a thoufand times more fit, and more advantageous for *Peppa*, than with a *Spaniard*, of whom they had no knowledge, either of his Eftate or Family, that at laft the Prince *Doria* remain'd fatisfy'd, and promis'd his Wife never to confent that his Daughter fhould marry the Marquefs of *Villa Mediana*. In the mean while, the Princefs *Doria* was refolv'd not to defer any longer the fpeaking to *Peppa* in behalf of her Nephew, and fhew'd her the Letter fhe had receiv'd from him. *Peppa*, hiding part of her Refentment, anfwer'd her coldly, That her Honour

E   had

had been too fenfibly touch'd to hearken to a Man that had once not
efteem'd her worthy of him. The
Princefs judging it not convenient to
prefs her any further, imagining that fhe
fhould find fome means in length of time
to vanquifh this nice Punctilio.

As the Marquefs of *Villa Mediana* had
writ to *Spain*, that *Peppa* would not be
forry to have him, and had the vanity
to add feveral things to his advantage,
the Prince *Doria* near that time had a
Letter from a *Genoefe* that was his
Friend, who refided at *Madrid*. He
gave him an account, that he had heard
talk of the offer that was made him to
marry his Daughter to the Marquefs of
Villa Mediana, and how he alfo knew
that the King of *Spain* us'd his Intereft
in the cafe; that thereupon he could
not forbear counfelling him as a Friend,
that if he aim'd at the Quiet and Satisfaction of his Family, he ought not to
oppofe this Marriage, being inform'd
from good Hands, that the Marquefs
had before hand poffefs'd himfelf of
the good liking of his Daughter, and
that therefore he ought, as a wife man,
to confent handfomely to a thing that
he could not eafily hinder.

The

The Prince *Doria* receiv'd this Letter with all the Regret and Despair of a Father, who has but one only Daughter, in whose Education he has taken great care, and who nevertheless disposes of her self without his share in the Approbation. Not knowing where to lay the blame, he complain'd of his Misfortune to his Wife, and reproach'd her, in shewing her this Letter, with the Liberty that she had given to his Daughter. The Princess had no longer occasion of surprize at the Answer that *Peppa* made her, when she spoke to her of her Nephew. She advis'd her Husband to dissemble his Anger, and cunningly to endeavour to procure from *Peppa* a Confession of the Truth. *Doria* went directly into his Daughters Chamber, and after he had exaggerated the Kindness that he had for her, the Care he had observ'd in her Education, and the Pains that he had taken, not only to conserve the Inheritance of his Fathers, but even to augment it; he told her that notwithstanding such manifest Obligations, he was inform'd from sure hands, that she had suffer'd her self to be led away by the subtilty of a Stranger. *Peppa* answering not a word to

E 2   this

this difcourfe, her Father continu'd to exhort her to conceal nothing from him, and promis'd her, that if fhe did deal ingenuoufly, he would pafs by all occafions of complaint againft her, and would let her fee, that he was very indulgent. *Peppa*, foftned by thefe words, and prepoffefs'd that her Father meant all this while the *Chevalier*, he being the fole perfon that fhe efteem'd worthy of her Love, thought that now fhe would make good ufe of the favourable Difpofition wherein fhe faw him, and cafting her felf at his Feet, her Eyes bath'd in Tears, fhe confefs'd, that it was true, fhe did love. Her Father interrupted her, without giving her the time to explain her felf any further, and after having reprov'd her with the higheft Injuries and Reproaches, he return'd into his Wife's Chamber, for fear that in his Anger, he might be mov'd to any violent action againft his Daughter. He was fo tranfported with his Paffion, and at the fame time fo penetrated with grief, that he fell dangeroufly ill. All means were us'd for his Recovery, which being apply'd in time, did in a little while regain him his former health. His Wife, who every

day

day saw him extreamly animated a-
gainst his Daughter, promis'd him, that
if he would let her manage *Peppa* by a
Contrivance to marry the Marquess *Spinola*, that she would take such exact measures, that none should know
of it till 'twas done. *Doria*, not enduring the thoughts that a *Spaniard* should
force himself into his Alliance, and become Master of all his Fortune, in spight
of his endeavours to the contrary, declar'd, that he would take no farther
care what Son-in-law he had, provided that *Villa Mediana* was not the Man.
Soon after the Prince *Doria* being perfectly recover'd, his Wife, with his private consent, feign'd that she had made
a Vow to our Lady of *Loretto* for the
recovery of her Husband, and declar'd
that she would go for to acquit her self
of it. *Peppa*, who was very glad of this
Occasion, to shew that she was no less
forward than the Princess in the care
of her Father's Health, declar'd, that
it would be a great satisfaction to her
to accompany her in this Journey; and
they set out so secretly, that only the
Countess *Centurione* was advertis'd of
their departure.

E 3 The

The Princess *Doria* assur'd of her Husband's consent, and prepossess'd that *Peppa* had not any natural Aversion against the Marquess *Spinola*, altho she had still observ'd some trouble in her Carriage, resolv'd to finish cunningly the work that she had begun so many years ago, and having sent a Man in whom she could confide, to her Nephew, who was then at *Venice*, she sent him word, that it was time to conclude an Affair that the two Families equally desir'd ; that therefore, as *Peppa* was one of the richest Heiresses of *Italy*, and that new obstacles might probably arise to prevent his Marriage, she had determin'd, thereby to avoid all Inconveniencies, to bring *Peppa* with her to *Loretto*, to the end, that he might seize upon her at their return along the *Adriatick-shore*, where they must of necessity pass. She added, that it being usual to see Pirate-ships send their Pinnaces ashore, and take away by force whatsoever they meet with, she judg'd it fit that he should arm a little Frigat, and that he might not render himself odious to his Mistress by this Violence, if he appear'd in it, he should send a Pinnace ashore with eight or ten of his

Men

Men cloath'd like *Turks*, who might
beset a little before day, a lone Poule,
where she would lodge purposely ; and
that these Men, after having carried
them away, and led them into their Pinnace, should take care to terrify them
by all the appearances of a cruel Slave-
ry, and that the next morning betimes
the Marquess should pursue the Pinnace
with his little Frigat, and after a short
engagement should take it, and deliver them: That if he executed all this
with Judgment, *Peppa*, that was of the
Humour of the greatest part of young
Ladies, who are always overjoy'd to
have those that court them, do something for them that is extraordinary,
would be sensible of the Bravery that he
might shew in relieving her, and would
think her self very happy to fall into
his Hands, after having escap'd from
those of the *Turks* ; that thereupon he
should conduct her to *Venice*, where she
would take care to have a Priest ready
to marry them, whilst the Impression
of the great Service he had done in delivering her remain'd yet strong in her
Fancy.

The Marquess receiv'd this Project
with all the Joy imaginable , and as

E 4 Time

Time and the Advices which the Princefs had frequently given him, ferv'd
but to make him the more amorous, he
prepar'd all things on his fide to put in
execution. The Princefs always lodg'd
at her return in fmall ftragling Inns, to
bring her Project about. 'Twas in one
of thefe Houfes, between *Rimini* and *An-
cona,* that the counterfeit *Turks,* fent by
the Marquefs *Spinola,* put themfelves in
a pofture to feize upon the Princefs and
Peppa, and to carry them off. They
foon render'd themfelves Mafters of the
great Gate of the Inn, and having terrify'd the Servants by fome violent
Actions at their firft entrance, they
run up into the Princeffes Chamber,
who had her Daughter in the fame
Room with her, and rudely forc'd
them to drefs themfelves with fpeed.
The Princefs, who faw *Peppa* very much
alarm'd, began to counterfeit a Greatnefs of Mind, and exhorted her to fubmit to her Deftiny without murmuring,
affuring her, (by a kind of a Prophetick
Spirit) that Heaven would not abandon her.

The *Chevalier* of ——— who was juft
upon going to take a great Voyage at
Sea, was defirous to take leave of
his

his Miftrefs before he imbark'd. He
went Poft to *Genoa*, accompany'd with
one of his Friends; having underftood,
when they arriv'd, that *Peppa* was gone
to *Loretto*, he contian'd on his Journey, with defign to meet his Miftrefs,
fince his time would not permit him
to ftay for her at *Genoa*. He happen'd
to arrive very late at the Inn where
Peppa lodg'd that fame night that the
Counterfeit *Turks* were executing the
defign of carrying her away. As this
Project could not be put in execution
without fome noife, the *Chevalier*, and he
that accompanied him, being awak'd out
of their Sleep, ftarted up, and quickly
dreffing themfelves, follow'd them fo
clofe, that they came up with the Men
juft as they were preparing to carry off
the Ladies on board of their Pinnace.
They charg'd them with that Courage,
that thefe fuppos'd Pirates, who did
not expect to find fo fierce a Preventi-
on, left the Princefs and her Women,
and retir'd in diforder. However,
notwithftanding the Confufion they
were in, three of the ftrongeft, who
probably knew their Mafters Secret,
feiz'd *Peppa*, and fled in all hafte towards
their Pinnace. The *Chevalier* having o-

E 5   verheard

verheard her Voice, purſu'd them ſo
hard, and with ſo much Courage, that
he preſently diſabled two of them, and
went to run his Sword through the o-
ther, when that this wretch fell down,
and begg'd him to ſpare his Life, aſſu-
ring him, that he was no *Turk*, but
that he and his Companions were employ'd by the Marqueſs *Spinola*, who
had agreed with the Princeſs *Doria* to
ſteal away this fair perſon that he had
now deliver'd. *Peppa* was ſo troubled,
both with her Adventure, and with
what ſhe heard this fellow relate, that
ſhe ſcarce yet knew to whom ſhe was
oblig'd for her Liberty. She juſt began to thank her Deliverer in terms full
of Eſteem and Acknowledgment, when
ſhe diſcerned by the dawning of the
day, that ſhe ſpoke to the *Chevalier* of———. Never in ſo ſmall a
time was any one remov'd from a great
Terrour into a perfect Joy. A moment before ſhe thought her ſelf a Slave,
and whilſt her Mind was ſtill poſſeſs'd
with frightful Ideas, ſhe found her ſelf
in the Arms of a Lover belov'd. So a-
greeable a change is far more eaſie to
imagin than to expreſs. The *Chevalier* related to *Peppa,* that he came to
Genoa

Genoa with a defign to fee her, and
that not having time to expect her return from *Loretto*, he had determin'd
to meet her on the Road; that he
arriv'd laft night late in this Inn, where
his good Fortune had conducted him
fo opportunely; thereupon he offer'd
to carry her into *France*, to fecure her
from the Violence of her Relations.
Peppa imagining at firft, that the *Che-*
valier fpoke this only to prepare her
for a defign of forcing her out of the
Hands of her Father and Mother, let
him underftand, that her Father had
fome knowledge of his Paffion, and
told him, that fhe did not defpair of
gaining at laft his Confent for their mu-
tual happinefs; therefore fhe conjur'd
him not to deftroy the Merit of the
Service that he had now done her.
The *Chevalier*, who of all Lovers was
the moft refpectful, threw himfelf at
her Feet, and complain'd of the mean
Opinion fhe had of him, affuring her,
that he would rather die a thoufand
times, than to have the leaft thought
of difpleafing her. They continu'd,
faying a thoufand kind and paffionate
things to one another, and gave new
Affurances, that their Love fhould laft

with

with their Lives. The *Chevalier*, who
would not be known by the Princefs;
and who after he had broke her Meafures, would not have been very well
receiv'd by her, defir'd his Miftrefs to
permit him not to appear, and that after having conducted her fafe to the
Houfe where fhe had lodg'd, he might
remain undifcover'd, and following her
at fome diftance, might be her Guard
till fhe came to *Genoa*. *Peppa* acquiefc'd
in his Sentiments, and in parting, when
fhe perceiv'd fhe was juft arriv'd at the
Inn, fhe pray'd him to remember, that
working her fafety, was employing
himfelf for that perfon in the World
who defir'd moft to compleat his happinefs. The *Chevalier* had no fooner
left his Miftrefs, but he met immediately the Gentleman who had feconded
him in attacking the Counterfeit *Turks*.
This Gentleman, who had been troubled all this while for his abfence, told
him, that he had been careful to attend
the Princefs *Doria*, and to prevent any
ill ufuage that might have been offer'd
her during this Confufion, but fhe
fhew'd fo little Acknowledgment, that
far from thanking him, her difcourfe appear'd full of Difcontent, letting him
know

know that she was not at all oblig'd
to him for his having expos'd his Life
for her. This was no matter of surprise to the *Chevalier*, who presently
imparted to his Friend what he had
discover'd concerning the private Intelligence that was between the Princess and the Ravishers; and the Promise that he had made to this lovely
Creature, to be always near, during
the rest of the way to *Genoa*, that he
might be able to assist her, if there
should be made any further Attempt.

In the mean while the Princess *Doria*,
whom the *Chevalier*'s Friend carried
back to the Inn, and who feign'd in
the presence of her Women to be much
troubled, was comforted in her mind
for the Misfortune which had happen'd
to her Nephew's Men, being prepossef-
sed, as several Persons had assur'd her,
that they had carried *Peppa* off. She
began already to think of going immediately to *Venice*, to authorise the Marriage of her Daughter-in-Law, by her
Presence, and by the Consent of her
Father, which she had under his Hand,
when that *Peppa* enter'd the Room. At
first she appear'd in a very great astonishment; but as Ladies, and particularly

larly thofe in *Italy*, without any Difficulty at all can diffemble their real
Sentiments, the Princefs threw her felf
about her Daughters Neck, and out-
wardly fhew'd an extream Joy to fee
her efcap'd from fo great a danger.
Peppa, who conceal'd alfo what fhe had
heard, and who was ftill fenfibly touch'd
with what her Lover had juft related,
about his being forc'd to return immediately into *France*, embrac'd her Mother-in-Law, the Tears flowing from
her Eyes. They prefently parted from
hence, follow'd at fome diftance by the
Chevalier and his Friend.   While they
were on their Journey to *Genoa*, the
Marquefs of *Villa Mediana* made ufe of
all his induftry to gain the Prince *Doria* over to his fide.   He engag'd his
greateft Friend to fpeak to him in behalf of his Love, and made him fee fo
many advantages for his Family, and
chiefly for his own Perfon; that *Doria* was vex'd that he had given his confent to his Wife, to marry his Daughter to the Marquefs *Spinola*; but when
that he underftood by a Letter from the
Princefs, the unfortunate fuccefs of this
Project, he thought that Heav'n would
not permit this marriage, fince it rais'd

fo

fo many Difficulties, and now no longer fcrupl'd to give *Peppa* to the Marquefs of *Villa Mediana*, efpecially when
he reflected upon the agreeable furprize
this would be to his Daughter, by declaring to her fuch News, as he did
really believe would be pleafing.

As foon as the Princefs and *Peppa* were
return'd to *Genoa*, the *Chevalier* being
oblig'd to be at *Toulon* before the departure of the *Fleet*, quitted this beloved Place, without having fo much
time as to contrive an Enterview with
his fair Miftrefs. In the mean while
the Marquefs of *Villa Mediana*, who was
fatisfied of the good Intentions that
the Prince *Doria* had for him, appear'd
with a moft magnificent Livery, and
frequented all the Streets, and all Places where he believ'd he fhould fee
Peppa. As fhe was thus importun'd with
his Services, fhe took hold of all Opportunities to treat him ill, and was
fo malicious as to place her felf in the
Church fo, that the *Spaniard* could never fee her Face. The Princefs *Doria*
being inform'd by her Husband, of the
Defign that he had to marry *Peppa* to
this Gentleman, obferv'd feveral times,
that her Daughter-in-Law was always
careful

careful to avoid him, and that she appear'd to have an extream Aversion against him. She had much ado to comfort her self for not having succeeded in concluding the Marriage of her Nephew, and this Design running in her Head, the least matter rais'd her hopes. Therefore she gave an Account to her Husband, that *Peppa* seem'd very far from having any Inclinations for the Marquess of *Villa Mediana*. The Prince *Doria*, prepossess'd (as he thought) with the contrary by the confession of his Daughter, judg'd, as all Fathers are easily induc'd to flatter themselves, that *Peppa* us'd this constraint because she would not displease him. This suppos'd constraint so work'd upon him, that going thereupon to *Peppa*'s Chamber, he declar'd to her, that forgetting his own peculiar Interest, and not weighing what would be most advantageous for his Family, he had consider'd only of making her happy, and had determin'd in favour of the good will that she had for the Marquess of *Villa Mediana*, to marry her to this *Spaniard*. *Peppa* remain'd so amaz'd at a Discourse she so little expected, that it was impossible for her to answer one Word.

Word.. A Moment after she fell in a
Swoon upon her Bed. The Prince *Doria*, surpriz'd and troubl'd at the swoon-
ing of his Daughter, call'd for help;
Peppa's Women ran into her Assistance,
and the Princess came soon after. When
she saw that she was recover'd, she endeavour'd to console her by all the
ways of flattering and caressing, and at
length demanded of her from whence
this Fainting did proceed. *Peppa* own'd
that she never had a strong Aversion,
but against one only person, and that
nevertheless she was so unhappy, that
her Father had made choice of this
very same Person to make his Son-in-
Law. The Princess, after having assur'd
her that the Prince *Doria* would not use
such Violence to her Affections, went
towards her Husband, and blam'd
him very much for having driven his
Daughter into Despair, since that he
might have remember'd, how she had
already perceiv'd that *Peppa* had no
Inclinations for *Villa Mediana*. *Doria*,
who comprehended nothing of all this
that he heard, believ'd that his Wife,
who as she was ingenious and contriving,
had turn'd the Mind of his Daughter,
and had ingag'd her to prefer the Marquess

quefs *Spinola* before the *Spaniard*, which
confirm'd him in the Opinion that he
had already of the Inconftancy of the
greateft part of Women ; but he was
neverthelefs in a great Perplexity and
Doubt what meafures to take.

In the mean time, as the Senate did
not proceed to any Refolution to fatisfie the King of *France*, upon thofe
occafions of Complaint that he had
caus'd to be declar'd to the Republick, the *French* Envoy retir'd from
Genoa ; which rais'd cruel Apprehenfi-
ons in the Minds of the greateft part
of the Senators, efpecially fince they
came to know that there was fitting
out at *Toulon* a great Fleet, and that
all the Ships were loaded with a prodigious quantity of Bombs, Granadoes,
and Mortar-pieces. The Commonalty
maintain'd that all thefe great Prepa-
rations were made againft the *Algereens*,
whom the *French* defign'd to extermi-
nate. The greateft part of the *Genoefes* believ'd all this to be very probable ; befides they were fo poffeffed,
that it was a difficult matter for any
State to injure them, that they would
never believe that thefe forces were
preparing againft *Genoa* ; but the wifer
fort

fort who know that Kings do feldom
let Affronts go unpunifh'd, liv'd in
great fears, and were of Opinion that
they ought to accommodate the matter
with that King upon any Terms. The
publick Affairs employ'd every Body
fo hard, and private perfons were fo
affiduous at Council, and at the different Affemblies that were thereupon
fummon'd, that none had leifure to
think of their domeftick Affairs. The
Prince *Doria*, who was without contradiction one of the moft confiderable of
the City, was call'd every moment to
the Confultation of the Senate, and the
little Time that he had to himfelf, oblig'd him to defer his private Affairs.
He determin'd therefore, by the Counfel of his Wife, not to fix upon any
Refolution about the Marriage of his
Daughter, while thisBufinefs which concern'd the publick was not fully decided.

While the Affairs of *Genoa* were in
this Condition, *Peppa* liv'd in continual fears, encompafs'd with her Enemies, under the Authority of a Father,
who would facrifice her to a *Spaniard*,
and under a Mother-in-Law, who me-
ditated new Projects to betray her to
the

the Marquefs *Spinola*. Every thing was
fufpected by her, and at laft the publick Calamity became her private confolation; for the formidable Fleet that
the *French* fitted out, and the juft occafions of Complaint that the King had
againft the *Genoefes*, though a matter
of difquiet to all, was the only Subject of her joy, and the only thing that
nourifh'd her Hopes, becaufe that if
the *French* King became Mafter of *Genoa*, fhe fhould then have the Pleafure,
by loving the *Chevalier* of —— to be
affur'd before-hand of a Powerful Protector for her Family. As fhe could
not find one Perfon but what fpoke a-
gainft the *French*, fhe avoided all Converfation: Her Coufin to whom fhe dif-
clos'd her moft fecret thoughts, was
the only Perfon that fhe thought endu-
ed with Reafon, fince fhe condemn'd
not the *French*.

Much about that time they heard
that the *Divan* of *Algiers*, more cunning
then the Senate of *Genoa*, had made
his Peace with the King, without ftaying for new Marks of his Anger, and
that he had already fent away Embaf-
fadours, to ask this Monarch Pardon
for what was paft. This news put the

Genoefes quite into Defpair, no longer
doubting but that the Storm which
was gather'd about *Toulon*, would fall
upon their City. The Senate affem-
bled at all Hours in the Day; at every turn they were making new Propo-
fitions, but never came to any Conclufion. The *Wifeft* were of Opinion that it was beft to fend away Poft
an Embaffador to make their Submiffion to the King; others judg'd that
it was too late. The Envoy of *Spain*
hereupon arriv'd, promis'd them that
they fhould not want a Fleet bravely
mann'd, nor a Warlike Army: And
he would fend for all the Gold of
Peru for their Service. Although
their Counfels were very different,
they receiv'd however a *Spanifh* Regiment into the City, which the Go-
vernour of *Millan* fent thither. They
alfo recall'd all the Bandits, and as
much as the Confufion (wherein they
were) would permit them, they diftri-
buted through all Parts fuch Orders as were neceffary to put them in
a Condition of making a vigorous Re-
fiftance. In the mean time the moft
confiderable Perfons of the City, fent
their Wives and Children to *Millan*,
                                    and

and to the other neighbouring Villages. The Prince *Doria*, after having moſt tenderly embrac'd his Wife and his Daughter, would alſo have them take their Leave of *Genoa*, and gave them an Equipage more numerous than magnificent. He advis'd the Princeſs his Wife to retire either to *Millan*, or to *Turin*, which ſhe thought moſt convenient; and above all things recommended his Daughter to her Care. The Princeſs *Doria*, who had ſtill a deſign for her Nephew, and who fear'd the Authority of the Marqueſs of *Villa Mediana*, would not therefore go to *Millan*, leſt ſhe ſhould deliver her ſelf up into the Hands of the *Spaniards*. She retir'd to *Turin*, where ſhe had ſome Relations, believing as ſhe had Reaſon, that ſhe ſhould there have her Liberty more than at *Millan*. Soon after her Arrival, ſhe writ to the Marqueſs *Spinola*, who was ſtill at *Venice*, ſending him Word that ſhe impatiently expected him.

The Court of *Savoy*, which is without contradiction one of the moſt polite in all *Europe*, has been an inviolable
ble

ble Sanctuary for the Illustrious Unfortunate. It would be even a difficult matter to find a Stranger that was ever discontented with his Reception at *Turin*. The Officers of the *Portuguese* Fleet can testify, whether *Victor Amadeus* the Second, who now Reigns in *Savoy* and *Piedmont*, has degenerated from the Magnificency of his Ancestors; and of late, the Officers of the King of *France*'s Houshold, retir'd from *Chambray*, loaden with Presents, and so extreamly satisfy'd with their acting after an obliging manner, which doubl'd their value, that at their return, there was not one but what spoke the Elogies of the Duke of *Savoy*. This Prince had just espous'd *Madamoiselle*, the Offspring of many Kings, and to speak in a word, Daughter to *Monsieur* of *France*. Upon the Princess *Doria*'s arriving at *Turin*, the Duke, who knew her Merit and Quality, receiv'd her with all the marks of Esteem that she could wish or expect, and offer'd her very obligingly, all that was in his Power. *Peppa*, who did not want the Assistance of her Birth, to gain the Respects of all wheresoever she appear'd, was regarded by all the Nobility with

Admira-

Admiration. The Ladies perhaps could not see her without some Jealousie, whereof there was no great cause of wonder. Nevertheless she was not at any of the Diversions that the Duke of Savoy had prepar'd at the arrival of the Dutchess, because the Princess *Doria* pretended to a Preheminence which could not be granted her, without Injustice to several Ladies of extraordinary Quality, who were at the Court of *Savoy*. The Nobility, who would have been very glad to have seen *Peppa* at all the Entertainments, propos'd several Expedients, to satisfy the Princess *Doria*; but as it is much more easie to regulate the Interests of Princes, than the Ranks of Ladies, they found it impossible to bring it to a Conclusion. The disorder of the Affairs at *Genoa* serv'd well enough for a Pretence to excuse her absence from the Diversions of the Court; for there came news, that the *French* Fleet was before *Genoa*, that several Voluntiers had landed, and that after having made themselves Masters of the Fort of St. *Peter di Arena*, they had burnt those fine Country-Houses which were the Delight of the *Genoese*; that the Frigats warping close to the City, had

had caſt into it ſuch a prodigious quantity of Bombs and Granado's, that it
appear'd rather a *Mount-Etna* cover'd
with Flames, than that *Genoa* which was
nam'd *Genoa la ſuperba*; and in fine,
that the Conſternation was ſo great,
that ſeveral Families retir'd to the
Mountains, and abandon'd both their
Goods and their Houſes; eſteeming
themſelves happy if they could ſecure
their perſons ſafe, as well from the Fire,
as from the Banditti, who began to pil-
lage the City. There was added to all
theſe Circumſtances, that the *French* had
loſt ſeveral Voluntiers at their landing
before the Fort of St. *Peter di Arena*,
and that alſo a *Chevalier* of a very great
worth, who was one of the moſt conſi-
derable Officers of the Fleet had been
kill'd upon the place; and that he was
generally lamented by all the Army.
All this news was a ſenſible affliction to
the Princeſs *Doria*; but when that *Peppa* was inform'd of the loſs that the
French had receiv'd, and of the death
of a *Chevalier*, who was a perſon very
deſerving; her Love, which at this Report was allarm'd, made her tremble
for the Life of her Lover, and all the
Circumſtances that ſhe had heard of the
Merit of this Chevalier, and of the

ſorrow

forrow that every body fhew'd for his
lofs, encreas'd her Terrour. She privately retir'd, and before-hand gave
her felf wholly up to all the Emotions
of Grief, which a perfon that loves tenderly can be capable of at fuch a time.
She paft over two whole days without
mitigating in the leaft her trouble : Her
Grief oppref'd her in a very high degree, and altho fhe had ftill a fmall fpark
of hopes left her, believing that there
muft be feveral Officers of Merit in fo
great a Fleet as this of the King's, fhe
durft not however enquire of the Particulars of the News, fancying that whatfoever fhe fhould hear fpoke of the *Chevalier* that was dead could be apply'd
to none but her Lover. The Princefs
Doria , who would not be comforted
for the Misfortunes wherewith her
Country was oppref's'd, had not obferv'd the great Difturbance that *Peppa*
lay under. But feeing that fhe came not
out to receive the Ladies that vifited
them, fhe fent to her to come into her
Chamber for to hear the reading of a long
News-Letter in the prefence of feveral
perfons, giving an account of all that
had pafs'd at *Genoa*. Although *Peppa* had
refolv'd to prefer the cruelleft troubles
wherein fhe was, before the clearing
her

her Doubts, which might prove either very Tragical, or elſe very pleaſing, yet ſhe could not reſiſt her timerous and preſſing Curioſity to be inform'd of the deſtiny of her Lover. She enter'd her Mother-in-laws Chamber, where ſhe found ſeveral Ladies who impatiently expected her, but rather for to know the particulars of the Affairs of *Genoa.* The Princeſs *Doria* read her Letter, which confirm'd all that ſhe had heard before at *Turin.* They ſent her word, after the ſeveral Circumſtances of the *French* landing, that they had loſt upon the ſpot, ſeveral Officers, and that above all, they were extreamly afflicted for the loſs of the *Chevalier de Lhery,* who was a Gentleman much eſteem'd, and who upon all occaſions had given proof of his Valour and Conduct. This name which ſounded like that of the *Chevalier* of———, whether or no it was ill ſpelt in the Letter, or that the Princeſs pronounc'd it not well in *Italian,* caſt *Peppa* into ſuch an exceſs of Grief, that it depriv'd her of. her Senſes. She underſtood it to be the *Chevalier* of———, and at the ſame moment ſhe fainted away upon a Couch where ſhe ſat. The Ladies ran to her aſſiſtance, but had no ſuſpicion that the loſs of the

French

French was the caufe of her fainting, being perfwaded that *Peppa*, touch'd with the Relation of fo many Misfortunes, whereof the *French* Fleet had been the occafion at *Genoa*, was thereupon feiz'd with this weaknefs. They had much ado to recover her, and were forc'd at laft to call her Women to her, who having quickly undrefs'd her, put her to Bed. She was pierc'd to the Heart with this cruel News, and fell into fo violent a diforder, that fhe fpent feveral days with a carelefs Indifference for every thing, and almoft without any vifible Senfe ; and if there was fometimes a fmall interval from her excefs of Grief, 'twas only to make her the more tormentingly fenfible of her lofs. She reprov'd her felf, for her (as fhe thought) Indifference, for having ftill had the Courage to live, fince fhe could no longer doubt the death of her Lover ; fhe continu'd many days in thefe cruel ago-nies, but at laft, the force of her Youth furmounted fo far that of her Grief, as to permit her, when fhe had no Company in her Chamber, to pafs fome melancholy moments in breathing forth this Song.

Ome, come gentle Death,

and

and close these Eyes ; come stop

the Current of my Grief ; on you

my Rest relies, be quick with your

Relief : For by the chance of War

my Damon's laid, mangl'd and

bloody

bloody in his Grave: Oh God!

Oh God of Battel! No diſtinction

made between the Coward, and the

Brave! Zelinda weep, Zelinda

weep, until thy Tears drown both

thy

thy self, and all thy Cares; but

haften fooner, (oh ye Gods!) my

Doom, that I may fly, that I may

fly to Damon in his Tomb, to Da

mon in his Tomb.

The

The Princeſs *Doria*, who daily expected her Nephew, whom ſhe knew
was gone from *Venice*, left nothing
untried to manage the Inclinations of
Peppa, and although ſhe could not comprehend the Reaſon of the Deſpair
wherewith ſhe ſaw her oppreſs'd, ſhe
notwithſtanding acted with all imaginable Complaiſance. The Marqueſs
Spinola, being arriv'd at *Turin* about this
Time, went immediately to find his
Aunt, who receiv'd him with inexpreſ-
ſible Joy; but ſhe durſt not preſent him
to her Daughter-in-Law, in the Diſorder wherein ſhe then was. However
the next day after his Arrival, ſhe
would carry him to ſee *Peppa*, but be-
thinking her ſelf of the Anguiſh that
afflicted her, ſhe deſir'd the Marqueſs
to ſtay in the Anti-Chamber, whilſt ſhe
would go and prepare her to receive
him obligingly. She thereupon went
into *Peppa*'s Chamber, and after having
order'd the Women to withdraw that
ſerv'd her, ſhe told her that the Marqueſs *Spinola* was juſt arriv'd, that he
had paſs'd through *Genoa*, and that he
could give a more particular account of
every Accident that had happen'd there.
Peppa, who preſently perceiv'd that the
Princeſs aim'd at ſome new Deſign in
favour

favour of her Nephew, gave her not
time to proceed, but interrupting her
with Tears in her Eyes, told her that
she would now no longer make a Secret
of her Inclinations which she had hid
till then, since also she had now nothing
more to trust to, being resolv'd to de-
prive her self of Worldly Converse,
which was become insupportable to
her. She then declar'd that she had
all along had some Inclination for the
Chevalier of——since they saw one
another at the Ball, that was given at
the Palace of the Marquess *Justiniani*;
that Sympathy had work'd the same
Effect upon the mind of the *Chevalier*
who retir'd into *France*, for to avoid
the Consequence of this Inclination,
which forc'd him to love in spite of all
his Resolution ; that they had run o-
ver two years without either seeing or
knowing one another till the time that
the Marquess *Spinola* being by chance
return'd from *Rome* with the *Chevalier*
of——had conducted him to their House,
and so had unknowingly given them the
Opportunity to revive their first Sentiments, to declare a-new their Affections, and to love with a Passion most
violent and lasting ; that in the end,
their Love had taught them an Expedient

dient both to fee, and to Write to one
another, as well as to exchange on
both fides an Affurance to continue firm
in their Sentiments. 'Twas he, added
*Peppa, that arriv'd fo opportunely in the
way to* Loretto, *as to deliver me from the
Turks, who were not what they appear'd, for
one of them confefs'd to us, that they were
employ'd by your Nephew, who had privately agreed with you, to carry me off by
force. I never yet fpoke to you of it, becaufe being affur'd of the Conftancy of
my Lover, all other things gave me not the
leaft trouble. I ftill flatter'd my felf with
the Hopes that the Senate would make their
Peace with the King of* France, *and that
that might facilitate our Marriage ; but
all thefe flattering hopes are vanifh'd, and
I now propofe to my felf no other Confolation but that of lamenting the Lofs of my
Lover, all the reft of my Life.* She pour'd
forth a Flood of Tears, in uttering thefe
laft words. Neverthelefs fhe continu'd
her Difcourfe, and told the Princefs
that fhe was refolv'd to go throw her
felf at the feet of the Dutchefs, to in-
treat her Protection, and to beg that
fhe might be receiv'd into the Society
of the Nuns of the Annunciation. However, if after the Confeffion that fhe had
made, there remain'd yet in her Breaft
fome

some Sentiments of Compaſſion for her,
ſhe might if ſhe pleas'd eaſily ſave her
the Confuſion that would ſeize her when
ſhe went to inform ſo great a Princeſs
of her weakneſs, and prevent her becoming the talk of all the Court ; where-
fore ſhe expected this promiſe from her,
that ſhe might be conducted to this Convent wherein ſhe deſir'd to enter without
ſtaying for her Father's Orders. The
Princeſs melted into Tears at her Relation, and had ſcarce the Force either
to blame her weakneſs, or to make her
ſenſible that ſhe ſhar'd in her Grief. She
at laſt aſſur'd her, that ſhe would contribute to her ſatisfaction as far as poſſible ſhe could, and went out to entertain the Marqueſs *Spinola*, who had o-
verheard all their Converſation, and
who was ſo ſenſibly afflicted with Grief
at the Recital *Peppa* had made, that
'twas not difficult to be diſcern'd when
the Princeſs came to him. He was infinitely concern'd to have bin thus long
a Pretext to his Aunt for oppoſing a
Paſſion both ſo real and ſo tender. He
was then of the mind that if he had
but known how conformable were the
Sentiments of *Peppa* and the *Chevalier*,
he would have taken no ſmall delight in
ſerving them and favouring their deſign. The Princeſs was extreamly ſurpris'd

pris'd to find her Nephew in this condition, but she was much more so, when
he told her that he heard all that *Peppa*
had said to her, and that he was sensibly griev'd, as well for the Sorrow
she endur'd, as for the Death of the
Chevalier. He mention'd him with the
greatest marks of Esteem, and com-
plained to his Aunt of the trouble that
she had given the two Lovers. The Princess assur'd him that she never had any
Knowlege of their Passion, and told him
further, that in the condition wherein
Affairs were then, she would have advis'd her Husband not to refuse the *Che-*
valier his Daughter, since that he lov'd
her so entirely, because it might very probably come to pass that if the Senate did
not find some Means to appease the King,
this Monarch would reduce the whole
State of *Genoa* under his Subjection.

In the mean time the *Chevalier* of-—
being inform'd that his Mistress was at
Turin, immediately took post thither:
As soon as he was landed, he happen'd
by chance to stop at the same house
where the Marquess *Spinola* lodg'd. Our
Marquess presently knew him, and was
so surpris'd to see a man whom he was
inform'd was dead, that he look'd at
him several times without saluting him,
imagining that he was mistaken by the

Resem

Refemblance of fome Features. The *Chevalier*, who judg'd by the furprize of the
Marquefs that he had knowledge of his
Paffion, did not forbear coming up to
him, and faluting him very civilly. He
then told him, that he was perfwaded
that the fame Affair was the caufe of both
their Journeys to *Turin.* The Marquefs
recalling himfelf out of the Surprife he
was in, return'd the Complement to the
Chevalier, and declar'd to him that (wa-
ving whether or no they came both upon
the fame Errand,) he knew, that for his
part, he efteem'd no Bufinefs more important, then the care he always took to
contribute to his happinefs. He gave him
an Account of the Report that was
fpread abroad of his Death, by what
means he had heard the particulars of
his Love towards his own Miftrefs, of
the defpair *Peppa* was in, and of the
extraordinary Refolution that fhe had taken, to leave the World, and to fhut her
felf up for ever in a Convent. The *Chevalier* hearken'd with infinite fatisfaction
to *Peppa*'s Refolution, which fufficient-
ciently juftified the Strength of her Paffion ; but having heard that fhe was fick,
and that no body was permitted to enter
into her Chamber, he believ'd it a very
difficult thing for him to fee her, efpecially

ally having the Princefs *Doria* againft
him, who had in Profpect what was wholly oppofite to his Love.   The Marquefs
left him ftill in his Error, and without
letting him know that the Princefs would
be more favourable to him than he could
imagine, he only promis'd him that he
would find out fome means to introduce
him fecretly to *Peppa*. This Promife put
the *Chevalier* into a great Extafie. He
embrac'd the Marquefs, who left him to
go fpeak to the Princefs. She appear'd
to him much concern'd that *Peppa* ftill
perfifted in her firft Refolution, and was
continually preffing her to be carried to
the Nunnery of the Annunciation. The
Marquefs told her that he was juft come
from a Gentleman whom he had known
at *Rome* and whofe fame was very great
for his Ability in curing any Diftemper
of the Mind, and that if fhe pleas'd, he
would bring him that he might give his
Opinion of the defpair and trouble which
Peppa labour'd under ; and he would affure her before hand, that this Gentleman would diminifh much of her trouble
affoon as ever he had but fpoke to her.
The Princefs who was ftill far from fufpecting the Miftery that the Marquefs
hid from her, conjur'd him to bring this
Gentleman the very fame day. She ad-
                                        ded

ded so many things concerning the Joy
she should receive, if she could but give
Peppa as great an occasion now to commend her, as formerly she had reason
to be displeas'd, that the Marquess *Spinola* thought he might no longer dissemble the happy Rencounter that he had
made. He was resolv'd however to know,
before he told her that the *Chevalier*
was living, if she would really favour his
Passion, as she declar'd how much she
wish'd to have been made sensible of it
before. He turn'd the Discourse to the
Affairs of *Genoa*; and after he had ex-
agerated the Importance thereof, he told
her that he had heard from very good
hands, that a general Peace was agreed
on, none having had so much care for the
Interest of the Republick, as to see that
Genoa should be included, the *French* King
having reserv'd to himself what punish-
ment he had design'd them, that this
caus'd in him a great deal of Fear for his
Countrey, and she might hereby see that
the Marriage of *Peppa* with the *Chevalier*
of——would have been very advantageous to her Family. The Princess who
admitted all these Reasons of her Nephew to be very substantial, assur'd him
that she should not have oppos'd it, if
the Correspondence that the *Chevalier*

had

had with *Peppa*, had but been known to her. *Since that you are in this mind,* replied the Marquefs, *it depends now upon you to oblige the Republick with a Protector, who has no small Power in the French Court, and engage* Peppa *to you by an everlasting Acknowledgement, and to do an Action which will Crown you with Glory.* The Chevalier of ——*is not dead; and to conceal nothing from you, 'tis he that I intend to bring to* Peppa, *under the name of the Gentleman of* Rome, *who is Master of such great Secrets in Physick. The Interest of our Republick, as well as the Esteem that I have for him, perswades me to propose to him that he should marry* Peppa *privately; and methinks by all the Reasons which I have urg'd, you must needs receive a great satisfaction in being favourable to the Passion of two Persons who have lov'd so long and so tenderly.* Altho' the Princefs *Doria* was convinc'd with thefe Reafons of her Nephew, fhe was notwithftanding in a great Perplexity. She fear'd to take upon her an Affair fo nice; but the Marquefs ftill alledg'd fo many Reafons, and fo earneftly beg'd her to grant him the Favour which he ask'd, that fhe promis'd at laft to confent to the Union of thefe two Lovers. She would however let *Peppa* take the Pleafure of the furprife, and told the

Marquefs

Marquefs that without letting her receive the leaft notice of the Truth, fhe
would propofe to her only to fee a Man
who would engage for her Recovery.
The Marquefs return'd to find out the
Chevalier, who upon the hopes of the Affiftance promis'd, did now fuffer a moft
tormenting Impatience for the fight of
him.   He affur'd him, that he fhould
quickly fee *Peppa*; and the Thanks that
he receiv'd for it, convinc'd him fo much
of the truePaffion he had for her, that he
believ'd he might now be plain with him.
He therefore councell'd him, fince that
he was fo much in Love, to think of contriving a fecret Marriage, and not to expofe any longer a Paffion fo true, fo reciprocal, and fo tender, to the uncertain
Events of Fortune, which might ftill produce new Obftacles.   He promis'd him
further, that he would make all the Intereft he could with the Princefs *Doria*,
in his Favour. The *Chevalier*, who durft
not have extended his Hopes fo far, was
charm'd with this Promife; and embracing the Marquefs, told him, That this
was giving him more than a Life, to obtain of the Princefs, that fhe would let
him marry *Peppa*. They continu'd a long
Converfation together, and the *Chevalier* fhew'd fo fervent a Paffion, that the
Marquefs

Marquefs had much a-do to forbear dif-
clefing what Sentiments the Princefs had
for him. Judge to what great excefs was
his Joy, when that the Marquefs having
gone out the next morning, return'd a
little while after, he told him, That he
had difcours'd with his Aunt, and that
having let her know that he was ftill not
only alive, but that it was his higheft Ambition to make *Peppa* fenfible of his Love,
by anyObligation whatfoever that might
be propos'd to him, he had found her
difpos'd to agree to all that he could expect. His Happinefs appear'd fo little
credible, that he was long in doubt, whether or no his Senfe of Hearing was as
good as it us'd to be. He made the Marquefs repeat over again feveral times the
Affurance he had given him of the Confent he had obtain'd of the Princefs. The
Service that he had done for him, exciting his Acknowledgments, made him
that he did not know how to leave off returning Thanks, which he exprefs'd with
a Zeal that fufficiently teftify'd the
ftrength of his Paffion. It was indeed too
violent, to let him defer any longer the
feeing of the Princefs *Doria*. He conjur'd
the Marquefs to carry him to her, and he
had all the reafon in the World to be fatisfy'd with his Reception. She affur'd
him

him very-obligingly, That she would not
have perfwaded her Daughter-in-law to
marry her Nephew, but that she was ignorant that she was pre-engag'd ; and
that when she had heard of the fecret Intelligence that had paft between them,
she lamented his death, which put it out
of her Power to make amends for the
Difquiets whereof she had been the caufe.
She added, fmiling, That she much fear'd
that *Peppa* was not in a Humour to receive his Vifit; becaufe she had mention'd him as a Man admirable in curing
fuch Diftempers that all other Phyficians
had not the leaft Knowledge of; to
which all the Anfwer she receiv'd, was,
That far from admitting of a Cure, she
fhould die with Grief, if she did believe
her felf capable of receiving any Comfort. *I believe*, continu'd the Princefs,
fpeaking to the *Chevalier, that she remains ftill in the fame Refolution of not feeing you. I'll once more try if I can't fucceed this time, then you fhall ufe the Power
you have over her.* In fpeaking thefe
words she conducted the *Chevalier* to her
Daughter's Apartment; and leaving
him in the Anti-chamber with the Marquefs, she went in to *Peppa*, who had kept
her Bed two days. She in vain endeavour'd to make her confent to the Vifit
they

they came to make her. *Peppa* remain'd
all along obſtinate in refuſing. *It is not
juſt*, ſaid the Princeſs to her, *to have
that Complaiſance for you, as to let you die
without help.* At theſe words ſhe order'd
one of her Women, who waited, to introduce the Gentleman that was in the
Anti-chamber, and who had boaſted to
have a ſure Remedy for her Diſtemper.
Peppa, whom her Sorrow made always
wiſh to be alone, and who could not
comprehend, that there could be any Remedy for a troubled Mind, where the
Body ſuffer'd not, complain'd of the Violence that ſhe impos'd upon her; and
perceiving a Gentleman enter her Chamber, ſhe turn'd to the other ſide, without ſo much as looking on him, being reſolv'd to make no Anſwer to any of the
Queſtions that he might ask her about
her Illneſs. The Princeſs convinc'd more
and more of her real Grief, pleas'd her
ſelf with the thoughts of the ſudden
change that ſhe would find in her
condition ; and ſtepping towards the
*Chevalier, I'll leave you all alone with the
ſick perſon,* ſaid ſhe to him, *The reſtleſs
condition wherein her Diſeaſe has caſt her,
having made her averſe to all manner of Phy-
ſick, I perceive ſhe deſigns not to hearken to
you ; but I hope, that ſince you are maſter of
ſuch*

*fuch an infallible Secret, as I have heard
reported,* you have alfo *Skill enough to perfwade her to make ufe of it.* She went out
in faying that, to her Nephew, who attended in the Anti-chamber, till 'twas
time for him to come in. In the mean
while the *Chevalier* approach'd to the
Bed, where his Miftrefs lay, and for to
oblige her to turn towards him, *What,*
faid he to her, *canni all my earneft defires
of offering you my Service, merit fo much as
one look ? Have you fuch great reafon to
hate your life, that nothing in the World can
oblige you to preferve it ?*

Thefe words letting her hear a Voice
like that of her Lover, caft her into a
Diforder which is impoffible to defcribe,
fhe thruft forth a figh at the remembrance
of his lofs ; and not daring to believe
that the news of the *Chevalier's* death
was falfe, fhe remain'd ftill in the fame
condition, without looking towards him
that fpoke to her. *In the name of Goodnefs,* continu'd the *Chevalier, difdain not
my Care. What fatal Refolution foever you
have taken, perhaps you may change it, if
you will but admit of my Affiftance.* He
pronounc'd thefe words with an Accent
fo tender, that *Peppa* trembling, and in
diforder, turn'd at laft towards him, and
raifing her Eyes up to his Face, fhe knew
again

again all thofe Features, of which her
Heart was but too full. *You live then,*
faid fhe to him, with a feeble and unaf-
fur'd Voice, *may I believe my Eyes, and
am I not in a Dream? I do live,* anfwer'd
the *Chevalier, and while you fee that all my
Endeavours are to be with you, you would be
unjuft, if you did not believe, that I live
only for you.*

We muft no longer believe it poffible
to die with Joy, fince *Peppa* could fuffer
the Emotions which a fight fo dear, and
fo agreeable caus'd in her. The *Chevalier* tranfported with Love, told her in
the moft obliging and fofteft terms,
That he was not in a condition to demonftrate openly the greatnefs of his
Paffion, but he would facrifice to her his
All, and never part from her more. The
Liberty that now was permitted them to
fpeak without Conftraint, gave them the
opportunity of declaring what they
had fuffer'd for one another, they made
a thoufand Proteftations of an everlaft-
ing Conftancy; and their Converfation
had not been fo foon finifh'd upon a Subject fo inexhauftible, if the Princefs, who
was impatient to participate in their Satisfaction, had not entred with her Nephew. *Peppa* at that moment began to re-
flect upon what her Grief had often
made

made her speak in her hearing; the Remembrance hereof put her into a Confusion that would scarce let her look up. The Princess *Doria* dissipated this trouble, in declaring to her that she might follow the Dictates of her Heart, and that far from opposing the happy success of a Passion that she saw so well established, she brought her Nephew to her, who renouncing in favour of the *Chevalier* all the Pretensions that he had made formerly, came now to assure her that he aspir'd but to this only Advantage of being receiv'd as a Friend to them both. The Marquess *Spinola* confirm'd this Assurance by all that the most real and sincere Friendship can inspire in a generous Heart; and *Peppa* full of acknowledgement for so great an Instance, answer'd him with all the esteem that he could expect. The *Chevalier* who was owing to his Assistance for the favorable Sentiments of the Princess, express'd himself again to him in all the obliging things that could be said to a Friend to whom one is infinitely bound; And as his Passion made him protest that he would never more leave his lovely Mistress, the Princess *Doria* interrupted him, by letting him know, that for both their Interests his return to *France* was indispen-

sable

fable. She added, that, not to let him have any
juſt occaſion of being any longer diſquieted, ſhe
would have him marry her Daughter-in-law before his departure, not doubting but that after
the manner ſhe deſign'd to write to her Huſ-
band, ſhe ſhould eaſily gain his Conſent, which
was neceſſary thereto ; but that for ſeveral Reaſons which reſpected the one and the other, ſhe
judg'd it moſt proper, that this Marriage ſhould
be kept ſecret, and that they ſhould not declare it till after that the Affairs of the Republick were come to ſome Concluſion with the
King. It is very needleſs to ſay any thing of
the Joy that the two Lovers receiv'd from a
Propoſition which would raiſe them to ſuch a
State that was the final Obſect of all their
Wiſhes. The imagination of thoſe who never
had their hearts touch'd with Love, can't poſ-
ſibly penetrate far enough to conceive the ex-
tent of ſuch a joy. The Princeſs Doria wrote
to her Husband, and the Chevalier took upon
him the care of diſpatching a Courier to Genoa.
His quick return ſhew'd that 'twas Love gave
the Orders which were executed with ſo much
diligence. He brought the Conſent which they
expected, and the two Lovers enjoy'd the Pleaſure of being at laſt united, after ſo many Ob-
ſtacles with which their Paſſions had been
croſs'd.

F I N I S.

BOOKS Printed for, and Sold by W. Crook at the Green-Dragon without *Temple-Bar*, nigh *Devereux-Court*.

DIVINITY.

1. B*Revis Demonstratio*, being the Truth of the Christian Religion proved by Reason, in 12°. Price bound, 10*d*.

2. **The Protestant Religion the safe way to Salvation**; or an answer to a Book Entituled, *Mercy and Truth, &c.* Together with the *Apostolical* Institution of Episcopacy. As also **Nine Sermons** on Special Occasions; by *W. Chillingworth*, the 5*th*. Edition. To which is now added Mr. *Chillingworth*'s Reasons against Popery, to perswade Mr. *L.* to return again to the *Church of England*, in *fol.* price bound 14*s*.

3. Mr. *Chillingworth*'s Book as before made more generally useful, by *Mr. P.* with some Additions, in 4*to*. Price bound 7*s*.

4. The Doctrine of *Passive Obedience*, Delivered in a Sermon on the 30*th*. of *January*, by *J. Ellesby* of *Chiswick*, 4*to*. price 6*d*.

5. A Discourse about *Conscience*, in relating to both the Extreams of Popery and Fanaticism. *M.* in 4*to*. price 6*d*.

6. Mr. *W. Howell*'s Visitation Sermon before the late Bishop of *Chichester*, 4*to*. price 6*d*.

7. Dr. *G. Hascard* Dean of *Windsor* his Three Sermons, one upon the 5*th*. of *November*, the other two before several Lord Mayors, in 4*to*.

G   8. Mr.

Books Printed for W. Crook.

8. Mr. *Manyngham* Preacher of the Rolls, and Lecturer of the *Temple*, his **Six Sermons** Preached on Publick Occasions, whereof two of them are on Anniverſaries, in 4to. price bound 2s. 6d.

9. A Sermon Preached at the *Savoy*, by Monſieur *Des Eſcotais*, now Printed in *French* and *Engliſh*, Twelves.

10. *Hugo Grotius*'s *Catechiſm*, Greek, Latine, and Engliſh, with a Praxis to it of all the Greek words therein, in 8vo. price bound 2s.

11 *The Spirit of Prophesy*, proving that Chriſt and his Apoſtles were Prophets; written by the Directions, and recommended to the Preſs by the late Learned Dr. *Peter Gunning*, then Lord Biſhop of *Ely*, in 8vo. price bound 2s. 6d.

12. *The King-killing Doctrine of the Jeſuites* in a ſincere Diſcourſe to the *French* King, written by a Roman - Catholick - Gentleman, in 4to. price 1s.

13. *A modeſt Plea for the Clergy* of the Church of *England*, wherein is conſidered the Reaſons why they are contemned and ſlighted, in 8vo. price bound 1s. 6 d.

14 **An Introduction to the Holy Sacrament**, or a ſhort, plain and late way to the Communion-Table, being inſtructions for the worthy Receiving the *Lord's Supper*, Collected for, and familiarly addreſſed to every particular Communicant, by Dr. *L. Addiſon* Dean of *Litchfield*. To which is added the **Communicant's Aſſiſtant**, being a *Collection of Devotions* to be uſed **before, at, and after** the Receiving the *Holy Sacraments*; price plain bound 1s. guilt on the back 1s. 6d. This Book is alſo bound up with *Common-Prayers* of ſeveral Binding, ſold by *W. Crook*. 15. *The*

15. *The Case of Resistance* of the Supream Powers stated and resolved according to the Doctrine of the Holy Scriptures, by *W. Sherlock* D. D. in 8*vo.* price bound 2*s.*

16. *Two Discourses*, The first concerning *Truth*, the second shewing *Popery* the great Cause of Atheisme, by *T. Muyningham*, Preacher of the *Rolls*, and Lecturer of the *Temple.* 8*vo.* price bound 1*s. 6d.*

17. *The Souls Communion with her Saviour*, or the History of our *Blessed Lord Jesus Christ*, as it was written by the *Four Evangelists*, and now for the benefit of all pious and devout Christians digested into *Devotional Meditations*, by a Reverend Divine of the Church of *England* ; in 12°. price bound 1*s. 6d.*

18. Bishop *Sanderson's Sermons*, the last Edition, in *fol.* with his Life to it.

19. *The Duty* and *Benefit* of **Frequent Communion**, in a Sermon Preached at St. *Peter's* Church in *Lincoln*, upon *Passion-Sunday*, by *W. Leightonhouse*, late Fellow of *Lincoln-Colledge*, *Oxford*, in 4*to.* price 6*d.*

LAW.

1. *The Jurisdiction of the Authority of Court-Leets*, Court Barons, Court Marshalica's, *&c.* together with the most necessary learning of Tenures , *&c.* by *J. Kitchin* , 8*vo.* price bound 6*s.*

2. *Praxis Curiæ Admiralitatis Angliæ*, Author *F. Clarke*, in 12°. price bound 1*s.*

3. The Reports of *Hen. Hobard*, Ch. Just. in *fol.*, price bound 10*s.*

4. The

4. The *First*, *Second*, *Third* and *Fourth* Part of the **Institutes** of the *Laws of England*, being a Commentary on *Littleton*'s *Tenures*. An Exposition of the *Statutes*, Pleas of the Crown, and *Jurisdiction of Courts*, in 4 Parts, in 3 vol. in Folio.

5. *The Law of Charitable Uses Revised*, and much enlarged, with many Cases in Law both Antient and Modern, with the reading of Sir *Fr. Moor* upon the Statute of the 43*d.* of *Elizabeth*, digested by *G. Duke* Esquire.

6. *Officina Brevium*, select and approved forms of Judicial Writs and other process, with their Returns and Entries in the Court of *Common-Pleas*; as also special pleading to Writs, in Fol. price bound 12*s.*

7. *A Dialogue betwixt a Student and a Philosopher* about the Common Laws of *England*, by *Tho. Hobs* of *Malmsbury*, in 8*vo.*

8. The several *Statutes of Bankrupt*, with the Judges Resolutions thereon.

9. *The Compleat Clerk*, being forms of all Presidents and Conveyances &c. in 4to. price bound 12*s.*

10. *Les Reports des tres Honourable* Edw. *Seigneur* Lyttleton, *Baron de* Mounslow. *Custos de la Grand Seale* d'Angleterre, *& de ses Majeste plais Honourable Privy Councill en le Courts del Reigne de Roy* Charles I. in Fol. price bound 12*s.*

11. *The Compleat Sollicitor*, entring Clerk and *Attorney*, fully instructed in the Practice, Methods and Clerkship of all his Majesties Courts of *Equity and Common Law*, Superiour and Inferiour; as well those in *Westminster* and the City of *London*, and elsewhere through the *Kingdom* of *England*; a Collection more uniform and universally

verfally advantageous than any extant of
the fame kind, in 8vo. price bound 3 s. 6d.

12. *The Reports and Pleadings* to them of
the late Lord Chief Juftice Sir *Edmund Saun-
ders* Kt. in Fol. in Two Volumes.

13. *A new Book of Declarations*, and other
Pleadings, General and Special, in the moft u-
fual Actions in the Courts of King's Bench;
as alfo, a Choice Collection of fpecial *Writs*
and their Returns, together with Obfervations
in Pleading, Inftructing the Younger Clarks in
the Practice of that Court, *Printed from the
Original Manufcript out of Court-Hand, to prevent
the Errours that doth happen by the Tranferib-
ing*; to which is added **Appeals** of Murther
and *Mayhence*, with Pleadings thereon, which
no other Book of this kind hath, &c.
Collected, and drawn by *John Haufand*, Gent.
late of *Cl. Inn*, in Folio, price bound 10 s.

14. *Two Dialogues in Englifh*, between a Doctor
of Divinity, and a Student in the Laws of
England, of the *Grounds of the Laws*; in 8vo.
bound, price 2 s.

15. The *New Natura Brevium* of the moft
Reverend Judge Mr. *Anthony Fitzberbert*, Corrected and Revifed; whereunto is now added
the Authorities in Law, and fome other Cafes
and Notes by the Tranflatour, out of the *Year
Books*, and *Grand Abridgments* of the Law, with
a New and Exact Table of the moft material things contained therein, 8vo. price
bound 6 s.

16. *Reports D'afcuns Cafes (qui ont evenus
aux tems du Roy Henry le feptiéme de tres-heu-
reufe memoire, & du tres-illuftre Ray Henry le
huitiefme, & ne font comprifes deins les livres*

G 3   *des*

des termes, & Ans de mesmes les Rays) seliges
hors des papieres de Robert Keilway *Esq; par*
J. Croke *Sergeant al Ley, Jades Recorder del*
City de Londres & prolocuteur del meason des
Communes, &c. Ovesque les Reports d'ascuns
Cases prises per le Reverend Juge G. Dallison, &c.
& per G. Bendlo *Serjeant al Ley, &c. La*
tierce Edition un bellie de pluis que deux milles
Reference *aux autres livres Cy bien Antiens que*
Modern de la Ley, Folio, price bound 14 s.

17. *An Exact Abridgment of all the Statutes*
in Force and Use, from the beginning of
Magna Charta down to the Year 1689. com-
prised Alphabetically under their proper Heads
and Titles. In this Impreſſion, the year of
the *King,* and the Chapter of every *Act of*
Parliament. have been compared with the *Sta-*
tute Book at large, wherein many hundreds of
falſe References are corrected with great ex-
actneſs and care, to prevent the Reader's being miſ-led as he hath been in former Editions, 8vo. price bound 7 s.

18. All the 4 parts reprinted of *Leonard's*
Reports, Fol. together.

19. The 3 parts of *Bulstrodes Reports* reprinted,
in Fol. in one Volume.

20. *The Register of Writs,* new Printed, with
the *Digest of Writs* added to it, and ſeveral
New Writs in Fol.

HISTORY, &c.

1. *An Institution of General History,* or the
History of the World in Two Volumes, by
W. Howell,

Books Printed for *Will. Crook.*

W. Howell, Dr. *of Civil Laws*, and Chancellour of *Lincoln*, in Fol.

2. *Clelia*, the whole Romance, in Five Parts, written in *French*, now put into *English*, Fol.

3. *Scarron's Comical Romance*, being an Historical Account of a Company of *Stage-Players*, full of variety of *Novels*, rare *Adventures*, *Amorous Intreagues*, being Witty, Pleasant and Profitable for all that design Innocent Mirth, Fol. price bound 8 *s.*

4. *The whole Series of all that hath been Transacted in the House of Peers* concerning the Popish Plot in 1678, and 1679. wherein is contained the most material passages in both Houses of Parliament, relating to the full discovery thereof, in 8vo.

5. A *Copy of two Journals of the House of Commons. The first*, for the Sessions of Parliament begun at *Westminster* the 21*st* of *October* 1678. and continued to the 30*th* of *December* next following. *The Second*, of the Parliament begun at *Westminster* the 6*th* of *March* 1678. containing the Transactions from the first day of their Sitting to their Dissolution, in 8vo.

6. *Historical Collections*, or an exact Account of the Proceedings of the Four last Parliaments of Q. *Elizabeth*, of Famous Memory; wherein is contained the Compleat Journals both of the Lords and Commons, taken from the Original Records of their Houses; as also, the more particular behaviours of the worthy Members during all the last Notable Sessions, comprehending the Motions and Arguments of the Renowned and Learned Men of that time, as *Cecil*, *Bacon*, *Rawleigh*, *Egerton*, *Burleigh*, *Buckhurst*, *Walsingham*, *Hatton*, *Coke*, *Croke*, *Spelman*,

Spelman, &c. Laboriously and Faithfully Collected, by *Heywood Townsend* Esq; a Member in those Parliaments, in Fol.

7. *Megalopsichy,* A particular and exact Account of the last Seventeen years of Queen *Elizabeth*'s Reign, both Military and Civil; (being the former Journal of Queen *Elizabeth*'s Four last Parliaments) with *Sir W. Monson*'s Account of the Wars between *England* and *Spain,* with the Number of Ships and Commanders at that time; to which, at the end is added Dr. *Parrey*'s Trial and Execution for Treason against Queen *Elizabeth,* in Fol.

8. *The Connexion* being choice Collections of some principal matters in King *James* the First his Reign, which may serve to supply the vacancy betwixt Mr. *Townsend*'s and Mr. *Rushworth*'s Historical Collections, in 8vo. price 1 *s.* 6 *d.*

9. *The Historian's Guide,* or *Brittain's Remembrancer,* being a Summary of all the Actions, Exploits, Sieges, Battels, Designs, Attempts, Preferments, Honours, Changes, &c. and whatever else is worthy Notice, that hath happened in his Majesties Dominions, from the year 1600 to 1688 shewing the Year, Month, and Day of the Month in which each Action was done, price bound 1 *s.* 6 *d.*

10. *The Bucaniers of America,* or an Account of the most Remarkable Assaults committed of late years upon the Coasts of the *West Indies,* by the *Bucaniers* of the *English, Dutch,* and *French* in *Jamaica;* to which is added the Second Volume, containing the dangerous Voyages, and bold Attempts of
Captain

Captain *Bartholomew Sharp*, and others, in 4to.

11. Mr. *Tho. Hobs* of *Malmsbury*, his Translation of *Homer*'s *Illiad's* and *Oddisses* into English, with the Life of *Homer*, and a large Preface of the Virtues of Heroick Poesie.

12. Mr. *Hobs*, &c. his Poem in Latine and English, of the Wonders of the Peak in *Darby shire*, commonly called the *Devils Arse of Peak*.

13. Mr. *Hobs*, &c. His Four Tracts. *First Behemoth*, the History of the Causes of the Civil *Wars in England*, from the year 1640, to 1660, Printed from the *Author's own Copy*, never Printed (but with a thousand faults) before. with a defence of his *Leviathan*, against Bishop *A. Bramhall*, and a Narration of *Heresy*, &c. 8vo. price bound 5 s.

14. *Compendium Geographicum*, or a more exact, plain, and easie introduction into all *Geography*, than any yet extant, after the latest Discoveries or Alterations; very useful, especially to young Noblemen and Gentlemen, the like not printed before, with 2 *Alphabets* of the Names of Towns and Places, the one *Antient*, the other *Modern*, in 12°. price bound 1s.

15. *Moral Instructions of a Father to a Son*, upon his long Voyage, being an easie way to guide a young man to vertue, 12°. price bound 1s.

16. *The Court of Curiosity* being the most exact and Curious Book of *Dreams* and *Fortune-teller* that is extant, being much enlarged and explained in this new Edition, in 12°. price bound 1s. 6d.

17. *The Flower-Garden*, and compleat Vineyard, being an exact *Flower-Garden*, and a true manner of planting all sorts of *Vineyards*, in 12°. price bound 1s. 6d.   18. *A*

Books Printed for Wil. Crook.

18. *A Modern view of such Parts of Europe* that hath lately been, and still are the places of great Transactions, *viz. Italy* with all its Princes, *France* with all its Provinces, &c. *Germany* with the Dukedom of *Lorrain* and all the Electorates, *Spain* with all its Dominions, &c. with Curious Remarks of Antiquity, 8vo. price bound 2s. 6d. Printed, 1689.

19. *The Present State of the Jews*, 12° price 1s. 6d.

20. *The first Estate of Malandison*, in 8vo, by the same Author.

21. The Translation into English of all *Homer's Illiads and Odisses*, by *Tho. Hobs*, in 12°. price bound 5s.

22. *Brittains Glory, and Englands Bravery*, wherein is shewn the degrees of Honour from the Prince to the Pesant, with the honour of the Nobles, and Priviledge of the Commons, and the proper places and precedency of all Persons, from the Throne to the Bondman, more particularly in Coronations, Feasts, Funerals, &c. To which is added a *Continuation of the Historians Guide*, to *June* 1689. in 12°.

Alcander and Philocrates (Wing A884A) is reproduced courtesy of the Rare Book and Special Collections Library, University of Illinois at Urbana-Champaign. The text block of the original measures 6.7 × 12.6 cm.

We thank Professors Alvan Bregman and Bruce Swann for their assistance in attempting to reproduce sometimes too tightly-bound pages of this unique copy.

Readings where the copy is illegible or missing:

Title page   .1   ALCANDE[R]
               .2   AND
               .4   T[HE]
               .8   [A]
             .13 B[urrowes in Cornhill]
        12.2 Din'd
       87.4 [wo]man
      121   last line missing
      122   last line missing
      132.2 [assum']d
      132.3 [inter]rupted]

ALCANDER

AND

PHILOCRATES

w OR, T

Pleasures and *Disquietudes*

OF

MARRIAGE

NOVEL.

Written by a Young Lady.

LONDON, Printed for R. Baldwin
at the *Royal Exchange*, S. Mister at
vent-Garden, and S. Burrows in Covent
1696.

To the Right Honourable, the Earl of
ARRAN, Knight of the most
Ancient, and most Noble Order of
the THISTLE, &c.

TWas much much ado, my Lord, that I
resolv'd to prefix so great a Name to
such a Trifle; but I consider'd, that as
the truly generous chuse always the unfortunate and poor, for Subjects of their Generosity;
so it may be the Glory of illustrious Persons to im-
mortalize those Works by their Patronage, which
cou'd not by their own Worth support themselves:
And I was the more willing to throw this little
Book at your Lordship's Feet, that the shame of
having made your Lordship so mean a Present,
may incite me to some more noble Undertaking; by
way of atonement; and the Ambition of producing something of my own, less unworthy of your
Lordship's Protection, may inspire me beyond my
natural Genius. In the mean time, my Lord, that
I hope you will be pleas'd to look favourably on my
first Attempt in this kind, and not be too severe on
a Woman's Faults; next the two Heroes (if I may
call them so) of this Novel, beg your Lordship's
decision of their grand Dispute, whether it is best
to live single, or to marry; which tho' the only
Subject of this Piece, is left unresolv'd. And indeed, in my Opinion, they had before chosen a very improper, because an unexperienc'd Judge of
their Contest; but your Lordship, who has try'd
both Estates, will be best able to give a just Sentence.

of the Countess of Arran, will not doubt for which side you will determine; a Lady, so perfectly accomplish'd————but I dare not attempt to praise her, whose Name ought to be celebrated by all the noblest Pens, if her own Vertues did not give her a more certain Immortality.

And now, my Lord, our Expectations are on your Lordship, all wishing with Impatience that you wou'd make a second choice, one worthy to succeed that excellent and pious Princess, the present Dutchess of Hamilton, from whom we might hope for a young Inheritor of the Glory and Dignity of his great Ancestors, and of those Noble Vertues, which give your Lordship a more venerable Greatness than that which you derive from your illustrious Birth. Were I capable, my Lord, of doing Justice to your Merit, with what delight cou'd I dwell upon this glorious Theam, whilst I need not fear the Imputation of Flattery from any, since all Parties amidst their hottest Dissentions, agree in their value of your Lordship, those eminent Vertues, which their Interest wou'd make them Enemies to, forcing their Admiration.

This Contemplation draws me to a consideration of my Presumption in this Address, and makes me hasten to retire from so great a Presence, which I ought to stand more in awe of, than all the vain Censures of the Town, which I have shelter'd my self from with so much Care, being known by no Name but that which will be my Protection, the Title of,

My Lord,
    Your Lordship's most Oblig'd,
       Most Humble Servant.

ALCAN-

ALCANDER

AND

PHILOCRATES:

OR, THE

Pleasures and *Disquietudes*

OF

MARRIAGE.

*A*Lcander had no sooner heard that his Friend *Philocrates* was upon the point of Marriage, than he run to his Lodging, where he found him alone, with the Abbot *Sophis*. Your Friends (said he to him) will, without doubt, come to Rejoyce with you, for what you are going about; and I am come to tell you, that it distracts me. Unhap-

py Wretch ! into what Abyſs of Pains and
Diſquiets are you going to throw your
ſelf ? Marry ! (continued he) what Sin
have you committed to be puniſh'd with
ſo many Miſeries as are going to over-
whelm you, to engage your ſelf all your
Life to one Perſon, without being able to
change ? Let her become Sullen, Ugly,
Old, or Unfaithful, you muſt Die Chain'd
to her, or elſe proceed to ſcandalous Ex-
tremities. But you who talk at this rate,
(anſwer'd *Philocrates*, with an Air cold and
penſive) have not you been Marry'd, and
ſenſibly afflicted at the Death of your
Wife ? 'Tis very true, (reply'd *Alcander*) and yet I never ſuffer'd ſo much as in
the two years I paſs'd with her. How is
that poſſible (ſaid *Philocrates*) you lov'd
her, and ſhe you ? She was young and
handſom, had Wit, Quality, and Fortune, what then could hinder you from
being Happy ? I don't know what to ſay
to you, (return'd *Alcander*) but I am perſwaded, that let a Woman be never ſo
Amiable, or what ever tenderneſs one
may have for her, when one is become her
Husband, the Heart paſſes very ſoon from
Love to Indifference, and from Indifference to a Diſguſt. How comes that (reply'd *Philocrates*) ? I have a great ideal of
difficulty (interrupted *Alcander*) to pene-

trate into the true reason of it , it may be ; that in seeing a Woman very often, and more nearly, we find no more in her that Merit, and those Charms, by which we were attracted. It may be, the Heart does not agree with such a calm possession , or, it may be, in fine, that the frequent commerce of the Senses, extinguishes their vivacity. You drive things much too far, (interrupted *Philocrates*) a Man of Prudence, and Judgment, will not Marry a Woman without knowing her to have Virtue, and Merit ; so that the more he sees her, the more he discovers her good Qualities, and is the more satisfy'd with his Choice. He makes a duty, and a soft habitude of loving her ; she gives him a thousand innocent Pleasures, she keeps him from Debauchery, with voluptuous Lawful Joys ; she brings him fine Children, which she educates with tender Care ; she follows him in his Adversity, as well as in his highest Fortune. In fine, she is a faithful Companion, who never abandons him till Death. How shall one know a Woman before one Marries her ? (interrupted *Alcander* in a rallying tone.) Women are incomprehensible; the cunningest, and most penetrating, are deceiv'd in 'em ; they never speak or act sincerely, there's nothing but Disguise and Artifice in all they do ; they change without reason ; have no solidity in their Wit, or in their Heart ; their Beauty is not proof against a little Fever, nor their Virtue against the smallest Interest, or Pleasure. When they marry, they have only, for the most part, a certain blind, and irregular Love for their Husbands, which ceases in a little time, by changing its Object ; an insupportable Vanity, and Ambition, or a low a sordid Interest, is what takes up all their Thoughts. In the mean while, you wou'd have a Husband frame in himself, a soft habitude of loving a Woman with these faults, because he has Marry'd her ; believe me, the Heart is too great a Libertine, to subject it self to such sort of Laws ; to pretend that a Woman can retain her Husband by the Pleasures of the Senses, what probability ? For him, she has only dull, and insipid Pleasures ; if the Husband has a Penchant to Incontinence, she serves, at most, to nourish Fires, which he generally extinguishes in other places. 'Tis a fine satisfaction to have a Woman eternally by one's side, for whom one feels nothing but a disgust, or, at least an indifference ; a covetous or an imperious Woman, who Criticizes even upon your least actions ; or, a Fool, who fatigues you with her false Reasonings ;

a Coquet, an ambitious Woman, or a Gamester, who torments you with her extravagant Expences; don't deceive your self, there are few Women who have not that defect. For Children, what pains, what trouble, is not one at in bringing them up ? To how many Infirmities and Sicknesses are they subject ? And when they are grown up, what disquietudes to settle them in the World ? Sometimes they happen to be False, Debauchees, Unnatural, Prodigal, Imprudent, Gamesters; in fine, they are Inhumane Creditors, who take away your Fortune, and put you out of a condition to bestow it on your Pleasures. Why then (reply'd *Philocrates*) does all the World Marry, if that State is so uneasie? Some (answer'd *Alcander*) out of a motive of Religion, others of Interest, some for Policy, and others because the rest of the World Marry without examining any further. You deceive your self (reply'd *Philocrates*) the effects of Marriage are not so uneasie as you say, nor all Women so terrible as you would have us believe, the Person with whom I engage my self, is of a humour very opposite to those Women you have describ'd. Yes, *Fraudelisa* is nothing but Sincerity, and Virtue, a thousand Charms shine in her Soul, a thousand Beauties in her Per-

son.

fob, which are not to be seen in any other.
Philabell lov'd her to madness, and tho' he
is a Man of Quality, very handsom, with
a great deal of Wit, Gallant, and naturally belov'd by Women, yet she cou'd
not endure him, and refus'd to let him
continue his Visits to her, because of the
Liberties he took, and his Discourses with
double meanings : The poor Child told
me, that in one Afternoon he made her
blush twenty times.. She is not like the
Women of the Age, she loves retirement,
and solitude ; her Clothes, and all her Behaviour, is extreamly modest ; she never
lays out any thing extraordinary, but, with
regret, hardly knows the Cards ; and is
so far from all Coquettry, that t'other
day, I could not perswade her that any
Women could be unfaithful to their Husbands. I may say, she loves me tenderly,
and yet, whenever her inclination moves
her to give me some marks of it, her reservedness, and modesty, retains her.
Ah! how happy are we going to be (continued he) by our Marriage? Absolute
Masters of one another's Hearts, and Persons. We may, without scruple, and
without Partners, satisfie, every day, our
tender, Amorous Transports. Tender
and Amorous Transports (reply'd *Alcander*) are not Messes for married People.
And

And for whom then, (interrupted *Phila-crates*, raising his voice) for your *Lesbia*? for you? Believe me, (continued he) un-less we esteem a Woman for her Virtue, and her Fidelity, she can give us nore of the real joys of Love; those are but De-baucheries, in which the Senses alone find any Pleasures, without the Souls parta-king of 'em, which is the reason that they are generally follow'd with nothing but regret, despisings, and disgusts. How can one esteem a Woman (continued he) and rely upon her Fidelity, at the very time when she betrays her Duty, her Ho-nour, and her Religion, to abandon her self to her Passion? Ah! (reply'd *Alexan-der*) if you knew *Lesbia* as well as I do, how differently won'd you talk? Oh, there is not a Maid in *France* less Interested, or more Generous; she keeps two thousand *Lewis d'Ores* for me, with the last Fidelity; what Wives can be so trusted? *Lesbia* love Libertin sm! Ah, how far is she from it? She hates all Men, she loves nothing but me; and if she relishes any Pleasure, 'tis but with reference to me. And as far as I am sensible of it, I have heard her say a thousand times, That she won'd place her greatest felicity in seeing her self with me alone, in some remote corner of the World. I gave her the fine Ruby you

have

have seen me wear; she wou'd not have
taken it, and I had the greatest difficulty
imaginable to oblige her to it. It drop'd
out of the Ring and was lost; what tears
she shed! She wou'd have giv'n all she had
in the World to have found it, not that
she regretted it for the value, but because
she fancy'd it an Omen of my ceasing to
love her. This Ruby, said she to me,
which seem'd so fix'd, thus fall'n from the
Ring, can be no other than a sign, and a
presage, that I shall lose your love; but,
be assur'd, I never shall survive it. Can
you, in Marriage, find these Niceties, and
such a tender Passion? Marry'd People are
certain that they can never leave one another, and that assurance is the Poyson of
tenderness; Love cannot live without desires, without some fears, and some difficulties. Softly, softly, (interrupted the
Abbot *Sophin*) no comparisons with Marriage, bear it respect: I don't speak (reply'd *Alcander*, with a serious Air) of
those sort of Marry'd People who are entirely loosned from their Senses, and only
animated with a Spirit of Sanctity, and
Purity, but of those who engage in Marriage only to satisfy their Sensuality; and
who, not changing their Manners in so
holy a State as that of Marriage, are guilty
of abominable Adulteries, and so make
                                themselves

themselves a thousand times more criminal. *Philocrates* (interrupting *Alcander*) ask'd the Abbot which side he wou'd take; adding. That he had known several Abbots who wou'd have been very well pleas'd to have had it in their power to Marry. *Alcander* maintain'd on his side, That there were many Marry'd People who wou'd gladly change their Wives for Benifices. The Abbot represented to them, That none are ever contented with their own condition, that therefore they ought not to decide their dispute by that; but that, to judge of it solidly, they shou'd examine, with application, the Pleasures and Disquietudes of Marriage; that *Paris* was a great Theatre; that they need only hear the general Discourse; and, with the least Address, to turn their Conversation upon that Subject, it wou'd be easie to Instruct themselves very much in it in a little time. This Proposition seem'd very reasonable, both to *Philocrates* and *Alcander*; they intreated the Abbot not to leave them, telling him, They chose him for Judge; which he accepted. *Alcander* told them, that he must go first to a Bankers, about a business of consequence, whose Wife was of a singular, and pleasant humour, and that if they wou'd go with him, he cou'd promise them some diversion.

verfion. They agreed to it, and together
they went ; the Banker had juft D n'd,
and was in his Wives Chamber with her ;
but *Alcander* had no fooner begun to talk
with him, than one came to ask for him ;
he went out of the Chamber, and left the
Company with his Wife. *Philocrates* finding her young and fprightly, ask'd her
what Book fhe had in her Hand ; 'tis the
Princefs of *Cleves* (faid fhe.) What think
you of it, Madam, (anfwer'd *Alcander*?)
I think her very foolifh, (reply'd fhe)
what Impertinence, for a Woman to tell
her Husband that fhe loves another Man ?
Where had the Author left his Judgment
when he writ that Part, for he manages
the reft of his Subject well enough ? For
my part, (reply'd *Philocrates*) I can't condemn that, fince Madam *de Cleves* had a
violent inclination for the Duke of *Ne-*
mours, which nothing but Abfence cou'd
Cure, and that fhe had no other way to
remove her felf from him. Serioufly (continued he) if I had a Wife in Madam *de*
Cleves condition, who fhou'd make me
fuch a confidence, 'twou'd give me a great
efteem for her. Ah, Sir, (reply'd the
Lady fmiling) what a Treafure are you
for a Wife ! let but thofe Sentiments be
known in *Paris*, and you may choofe where
you will. But, Madam, (interrupted the
Abbot)

Abbot) what wou'd you have had the
Princefs of *Cleves* do? Since fhe cou'd not
(reply'd the Lady) forbear loving Monfieur *de Nemours*, fhe had nothing to do
but take a method for the fatisfaction of
all three, which was to difcover her Affection to him, to take fecret Meafures
with him, that the Intrigue might make
no noife, and to Carefs the Prince of *Cleves*
more than fhe had done before, that he
might not fufpect her. How many cruel
torments had fhe fav'd her felf this way?
What ravifhing Pleafures had fhe given
her Lover and her felf? And, to conclude,
fhe had not occafion'd Monfieur *de Cleves's*
Death, like a Fool. *Philocrates*, and *Alcander*, thought her reafoning fo pleafant,
that they fell a laughing, and highly commending what fhe had faid, which fo extreamly pleas'd her, that fhe went on, faying, You muft own, Gentlemen, that many Authors ftray very far from Probability, and good Sence; witnefs the Author
of the Diforders of the *Baſſer*. The
Marquis *de Roziers* loves Madam *de Landro-
za* paffionately; fhe has not the Character
of a very fcrupulous Woman, fhe is ruin'd
by play; he gives her twelve hundred *Louis d'Ores*, fhe keeps the Money, and refufes him the Merchandize: Was ever any
thing fo ridiculous and impertinent as this
Story?

Story ? The Author has certainly very
little knowledge of the World, to be ignorant of what a Woman in necessity is capable of doing for twelve hundred *Louis
d'Ores*. As she was talking thus, her Husband return'd from the Person whom he
had gone out to speak with, and having
heard what she had said, he gave her a severe reprehension for it, telling her, She
ought not to spend her time in reading
those sort of Books, but mind her Hus-
wifery and her House ; which nettled her
to that degree, that she said all she cou'd
imagine of most injurious to him. She
complain'd, that he was of a humour
Chagrin and Bizarre, that he lov'd Gaming, Drinking, and all Licentiousness,
that she had never had a Chamber-maid,
Old or Young, Handsom or Ugly, but he
had endeavour'd to corrupt them ; and, in
fine, to hear her speak, one wou'd have
thought him the worst of Men, and her
the wretchedst of Women. The Husband, on the other hand, reproach'd her
with the expence she put him to, in Jewels, and other Ornaments, the little Fortune she had brought him, the difficulty of
being paid it, her Gallantries, her making
Balls, her Masquerading, the Musick, and
Collations, she gave Her self at his Charge,
the number of People, of all sorts, which
she

fhe receiv'd at her Houſe to play ; made
her a hundred other reproaches, and ſaid
ſo many ſevere things to her, that they
had like to have come to blows ; but a
Footman, whom ſhe knew, coming into
the Chamber, made her forbear proceeding in her reſentments, to go ſpeak to him
in private ; he gave her a Letter, and
went preſently away, and for all the care
ſhe took to conceal it, *Philocrates* and *Alcander* perceiv'd it. Immediately ſhe went
into another Chamber, with an Air full of
Chagrin and Anger, and a moment after
out of the Houſe. *Alcander*, after having talk'd with the Banker of the buſineſs
he came for, went away too, with *Philocrates* and the Abbot, and going down,
Alcander found upon the Stairs a Letter,
in theſe words :

L E T T E R.

*Y O U promiſ'd me yeſterday, my Charmer,
that you won'd not at all ſuffer the Careſ-
ſes of your Jealous Tormenter laſt Night ; I
dare believe, how preſſing ſoever he may have
been, it being the beginning of the Spring,
that you have kept your Word with me. How
much am I oblig'd to you for it, my Dear ?
How ſenſible am I of it ! And how impatient*

to give you my Acknowledgments at the Place you know of !

As soon as they had read the Billet, they imagin'd it to be the same which they had seen the Footman give the Banker's Wife ; that it came from her Gallant ; that the Tormenter was her Husband ; and that the precipitation wherewith she had gone to the Rendezvous, had made her slip the Billet on one side, instead of putting it in her Pocket ; or that she had drop'd it in taking out her Handkerchief. *Alcander* thinking this example might be of use to his design, very coolly represented the unhappiness of this Man ; his Wife (said he) consumes the fruit of his Labours in wild Expences, she despises him, she makes an Academy of his House, she dishonours him, deceives him, and refuses him what a Wife owes her Husband, to make a sacrifice of it to her Gallant ! After this, be sure you Marry. Sincerely, had it not been a great happiness for this Banker to have had a Friend like me, that wou'd have represented to him what Marriage was, and have kept him from it ? Really (said *Philocrates* laughing) 'tis very pleasant in you, to draw a consequence from the conduct of Persons like these, in whom we see neither Prudence, nor good Manners ;

Manners ; what brutalities has not this Man been guilty of before us ? He knew his Wife to be of a violent Nature, why then did he provoke her ? Ought he not to have ftaid till he was alone with her, and fhe in a calmer temper, and then have told her what he had to fay to her ? Expofe his lewdnefs in his own Houfe ! rare Example of Virtue for a young Wife ! Faith (continued he) if fhe is unfaithful to him, he contributes very much to it : Believe me, a Man of Honour, who loves his Wife, who is affiduous, and careful of her, makes himfelf belov'd by her, makes her at once be happy, kind, and faithful. What then, (reply'd *Alexander*) you imagine there needs no more to make a Wife be happy, and faithful, than to love her, to have fome complaifance, and affiduities for her ; but you deceive your felf, (continued he) thofe marks of tendernefs, thofe affiduities, only make a Wife the more Imperious, and often gives her a difguft, and fcorn of her Husband ; witnefs the Marchionefs of *Seligny*, who is now Suing for a Divorce from her Husband. I have heard her fay, fhe fhould never have had fuch a thought if he had lov'd her lefs, and had been lefs affiduous about her. A very pleafant caufe of Separation (reply'd *Philocrates.*) She is

young

young, very handſom, and finely ſhap'd,
(ſaid *Alcander* interrupting him , ſome
Gown men, of the firſt Quality, are her
Lovers, by whoſe Intereſt ſhe obtains
what ſhe pleaſes ; and, in fine, ſhe has
manag'd ſo adroitly, that 'tis above two
years ſince ſhe liv'd with her Husband, and
that ſhe has been diverting her ſelf in *Paris*.
If you will (continued he) I'll carry you
to ſee her. *Philocrates* and the Abbot,
found the Ladies Character too ſingular,
not to have that curioſity. She receiv'd
them with a great deal of civility ; there
was with her, when they came, one of the
long Robe call'd *Berly*, and the Chevalier
———— As ſhe has always an extraordinary
deſire to talk of her Affair, *Alcander* had
not much difficulty to bring her to it.

Of all the Women (ſays ſhe) that ever
deſir'd to be parted from their Husbands,
none ever had more cauſe than I, nor ſo
much patience : Ah, miſerable Creature
that I am, (purſu'd ſhe) to what ſtrange
Deſtiny am I Born ! Other Women complain of their Husbands, and wou'd be ſeparated from them, becauſe they are ſo
far from loving them, and being often
with them, that they continually ſhun and
fly from them ; but my cruel Stars have
fix'd my misfortune in the troubleſom
Aſſiduities, and the exceſſive Love, my
Husband

Husband had for me. As foon as he faw
me at *Rheims*, he became defperately in
love ; his Perfon, his Eftate, and Quality, charm'd my Mother, and me by confequence, fo that the Marriage was foon
concluded. Prefently after he took me
from that engaging City, and carry'd me
to a place in the Country, which belong'd
to him, to give himfelf (faid he) entirely
to me. What I fuffer'd in that curs'd
place! He did not live with me freely,
and without ceremony, as Husbands do
with their Wives, there was nothing but
ridiculous Precautions, and impertinent
Cares, for what concern'd me; I muft not
think of rifing before Noon, my health
won'd be in danger. I had not the liberty to lie upon my Left Side, for (faid he)
the Liver is in danger ; and, upon your
Back, the Milt. What Vifions are thefe
to torment a Wife with ? I love Fruit extreamly, but yet I was not fuffer'd to eat
any, my ftomach was too weak. Walking I muft never think of; in the Day
time the Sun fpoils the Complexion ; the
Evening, and Night, makes one take
Cold, and brings Fluxions ; fo that I was
condemn'd to ftay all Day in my Chamber, working upon Tapeftry. Nay, for
the moft part, he won'd murmur againft
my Work too. For him he won'd pafs
the

the whole Day with his Eyes fix'd upon
me, sometimes complaining, and sometimes sighing. How charming are your
Eyes, Madam, (cry'd he?) Ah, that
lovely Mouth! Then, with a furious
Transport, he brought his great Lips upon my Eyes, and kiss'd them so hard, that
I was afraid he wou'd blind me. After
these first Extasies, he threw himself at my
Feet; forgive me Madam, oh forgive
(cry'd he) an insolent, audacious Man,
who ought to confine his Passion within
the bounds of respect and adoration! He
press'd my Knees till he made me cry out,
and then falling into a profound Melancholy, he gaz'd upon me with fiery languishing Eyes, and fetching deep sighs,
how much am I to be lamented (said he)
my cruel Fair one? You do not love me,
my company fatigues you, and you never
see me without being uneasie; alas, in
Marrying you, I thought my self the most
fortunate of Men, but now I find I am only the more unhappy. 'Tis true, I am
Master of your Person, but your Heart
won't render it self: Ah, ungrateful
Charmer, take back your Person, or give
me that cruel Heart! He did not end with
these first Transports: Well, Inhumane
Creature, (added he) since thou see'st the
violent Passion I have for thee, with indifference,

ference, and fcorn, here, (faid he to me
drawing his Sword, and giving it to me)
pierce, with a thoufand Wounds, this
Heart which thou doft fo much torment,
and end a Life which thou mak'ft fo infupportable to me.   This, Gentlemen,
was his Behaviour when ever we were together ; won't you own then, that never
any Woman endur'd fo much as I ? or had
more reafon to covet a Separation ? Did
he torment you, Madam, (faid *Alcander*)
as much in the Night as in the Day ? You
have a mind to laugh, Sir, (anfwer'd fhe)
but methinks I have made you underftand
enough. ⸱ This Saying was taken in a pleafant fence, that made all the Company
laugh ; then the Abbot taking up the Difcourfe, faid to her, Give me leave, Madam, to tell you, that he well deferv'd to
be pardon'd all his Tranfports, fince they
proceeded from his extraordinary love for
you, and his regrets for not being belov'd
by you. If he wou'd have made himfelf
be lov'd, (reply'd the Lady) he fhou'd
have obferv'd what wou'd pleafe me moft,
done all he cou'd to appear amiable in my
Eyes, and not have tir'd me with being
eternally in my company, and his infupportable way of behaviour. I love company, he ought not then to have taken
me from *Rheims*, but to have ftay'd and

entertain'd in his Houſe all the *Beaux monde* there, to divert me. I can paſs away ſome hours agreeably enough at Cards, ſo that he ſhou'd never have let me want Money, nor Company for play : Being well dreſs'd affects me, ſhou'd not he then have furniſh'd me every Month with all that was fineſt, and moſt faſhionable ? In fine, I love Diverſions, his chief buſineſs ſhou'd have been to procure 'em for me ; and that was the courſe he ſhou'd have taken to arrive at my Heart. Pray, Madam, *(*ſaid *Alcander)* how cou'd you contrive to free your ſelf from this Tyrant ? The moſt pleaſantly in the World (anſwer'd ſhe) : Near the Caſtle where I lived there was a little Wood, in which was found abundance of *Cantharides*, I got ſome of them, had them dry'd, and apply'd them to my Neck ; in a little time they made a great Excoriation, as I deſign'd. I feign'd my ſelf Sick, and acted ſo well, that ſometimes the Marquis found me ſighing, ſometimes looking up to Heaven as in deſpair ; and, at other times, in Tears, or a Praying.. I ſpoke to him of nothing but what was diſmal ; of Death, of Paradiſe, of Hell. In fine, I plaid my part ſo well, that I gave him a great curioſity to know from whence this change proceeded ; I foreſaw well enough, that he wou'd attribute it to some violent Passion I had conceiv'd for another ; and that he had too great a disposition for Jealousie to be free from it upon such an occasion : And I was not mistaken, he left no Artifice un-attempted to discover the truth. And one day, when he was condemning my Con-duct, with a great deal of sharpness, and complaining that I lov'd another, I threw my self at his Feet, and told him, That if my Life only was concern'd, I wou'd not make him a discovery, which, perhaps, wou'd give him a loathing for my Person ; but my Honour being in danger, by the injurious suspicions he had of me, I was constrain'd to tell him, That my Grand-mother had dy'd of a Cancer which had been neglected, that all our Family was subject to that Distemper, and that I had a long time felt some Symptoms of it, which was the cause of my appearing so cold, and so out of humour. In fine, that it had broke out, and was so extreamly painful to me, that I believ'd I had nothing to do but to prepare my self for Death. He wou'd needs see the Sore, which, after a little refusal, I suffer'd : The *Cantharides* had had such an effect, that he was deceiv'd ; he had never seen a Cancer, so that it was no difficult matter. Then I threw my self about his Neck, with tears in my Eyes, I

embrac'd him, gave him thofe fort of moving Adieus, which are ufual with dying
Perfons, and conjur'd him never to Marry
another after my Death. I fpoke to him
of a Will, and of a Feoffment in truft for
him. Good God! how naturally I feign'd
when I think of it ; if he was troubled at
my pretended Diftemper, he was as much
rejoyc'd to find himfelf, as he imagin'd, fo
well belov'd. Immediately he fent for
the Chirurgeon of his Village, who had
heard of Cancers, but had never feen any
no more than he ; fo that you may believe, it was eafie for me to perfwade him
that I had one. Monfieur *de Seligny* charg'd
him to take care of me, threatning, That
his Life fhould anfwer for mine ; which
feeing, he was extreamly frighted at.
I profited of that conjuncture, and, with
a little Money, perfwaded him to tell the
Marquis, that there was never a Man in
Provence, that knew how to Cure thofe
fort of Difeafes ; and that only one Phy-
fician in *Paris* had that fecret. I feem'd
averfe to the Journey, or, rather, I conceal'd the eager defire I had to make it,
telling him, I had rather ftay where I was,
and dye in his Arms. But I knew his
kindnefs too great to take me at my word ;
he rais'd a confiderable Sum of Money, and
conducted me hither, where I took Advice,

vice, feiz'd upon the Money, and left him
taking my Woman, and a Footman with
me. For the Form, my Counfel told me
muft give in a Complaint, wherein I
hou'd declare, That he had often drawn
is Sword againft me : Which I did. I
orgot to tell you, that at the time when
e play'd thofe Fooleries I fpoke of, to
you, when he drew his Sword in my
Chamber, I cry'd out, pretending to be
righted, which occafion'd my Woman
and Footman, to run in, and find him in
that pofture , fo that I made them both
Depofe, that they had feen him with his
aked Sword againft me. There needs no
more in Juftice to condemn him ; and my
Counfellor affures me, that I fhall infalli-
ay gain my Caufe. How much were you
to be lamented, Madam, (reply'd *Alcan-*
tr ?) but you muft own, that Monfieur
Seligny is no lefs unfortunate, and that
wou'd have been more for the repofe of
oth, that you had never married. Don't
ou perceive (faid *Philocrates*, addreffing
mfelf to *Alcander*) that the misfortune
roceeds only from the Marchionefs's ne-
er having had any Inclination for the
arquis ? and that if fhe had lov'd him,
eir marriage had been accompany'd with
ndernefs and pleafure ? It is not Love,
nterrupted *Alcander*) that makes a Hus-

B

band happy ; how many are there who suffer by the excess of love their Wives have for them? That's a thing extraordinary enough, (reply'd *Philocrates*) and which it will be hard for you to prove. I my self (reply'd *Berly*) know many examples of it, and I am perswaded that the Husband of a Coquet, who cares not at all for him, is less to be pity'd than one whose Wife dotes upon him extravagantly. How can that be (interrupted *Philocrates*)? A Coquet Wife (answer'd *Berly*) never contradicts her Husband, but is always of the same opinion with him, always gay, always endeavouring to divert him, and has every moment something new and pleasant to tell him. When he brings any of his Friends home, she receives them in the most obliging manner, she entertains them, and diverts her self with them ; if he caresses her she returns it ; if he seems cold, she neither frets, nor complains of it ; she has none of those delicacies of heart which serve only to make both unhappy, never any Jealousie, no uneasie humours ; if she has a Chamber-maid that her Husband likes, she won't turn her away for that : Let her defend her self, if she will, says she, let him attack well if he can, 'tis not my business ; whereas a Woman that loves her Husband extreamly, tires him Night

and Day, one while with her protesta-
tions of love and tenderhefs made out of
feafon, by and by with fufpicions and reproaches, and even fometimes with rail-
ings. *Valoury* has often told me, that
there is nothing fo infupportable as thefe
fort of Difcourfes from a Wife, for whom
the Heart is no longer fenfible, and that
he had but too much experienc'd it with
his ; fhe is always a crying, faid he, and
can hardly be made to take any nourifhment ; if I fail of coming home to Dinner,
or to Bed, fhe won't eat, and will fit up
all Night to wait for me ; fhe was once
very handfome, but with this fine way of
living fhe is become very frightful. After
this (faid *Valoury* to me) muft not you allow that I am the unhappieft Man alive in
a Wife, and that the Husband of a Coquet
is much lefs to be pity'd ? I have heard
(reply'd the Chevalier) of *Valoury*'s conduct with his Wife, 'tis fo highly ingrateful that he is not excufable in it ; fhe was
a Maid when he fell in love with her, his
Paffion made an impreffion upon her, and
fhe receiv'd his Addreffes, but being an only Child, and her Birth and Fortune above
his, her Father was againft it ; fhe lov'd
him to that degree, that fhe pretended to
be with Child by him ; there is nothing to
be imagin'd beyond the rigorous treatment

her Father gàve her, yet fhe remain'd firm
and conftant. In fine, the Father thinking there was no remedy, to repair the honour of the Family, confented to their
Marriage. This bafe Man had not liv'd a
Fortnight with her, (amiable as fhe was,
and tho' fhe had the laft tendernefs for
him) before he took a difguft for her, and
apply'd himfelf to another, much lefs de-
ferving than fhe. My God! how fottifh
you are, Madam *de Valoury*, (interrupted
briskly Madam *de Seligny?*) Ah! if your
Husband had had to do with me, how well
wou'd I have reduc'd him! What wou'd
you have done (reply'd *Alcander?*) When
a Man (replyed fhe) believes himfelf entirely poffefs'd of his Wife, and that he
has nothing to fear, nor to wifh beyond,
he quickly falls into an indifference for
her; 'tis that which made *Valoury* ceafe
to love his, feeing that he alone poffefs'd
her without a fharer. For my part, I
wou'd have acted more prudently than fhe
did, as foon as I had perceiv'd my Huf-
band's firft fondnefs for me abated, I
wou'd have made my felf fome Lovers,
whom I wou'd have brought to the Houfe
that he might fee them; Jealoufie wou'd
immediately have awakened his fleeping
Paffion, and reftor'd him to me. What
pleafure fhou'd I have had in affecting a
little

little cruelty, and rebuking him at first ?
I shou'd have made my felf a fecond good
Fortune for him; and thence it is (continued fhe) that Women who are adroit,
and gallant, are more belov'd by their
Husbands than others, becaufe, not finding themfelves in that tranquil poffeffion
which leads to indifference, they wifh, they
fear, they hope, defpair, and confolate
themfelves. And 'tis in thefe different agitations that Love nourifhes it felf; whereas the Husbands of Wives, of Madam
de Valoury's humour, and character, hardly return to their affection, becaufe they
don't feel that diverfity of movements,
their poffeffion being calm, peaceable, and
without trouble. Women (reply'd the
Chevalier) never want addrefs in the management of their amours; and after, what
Madam *de Valoury* has done, one may fay,
with reafon, that nothing is impoffible for
them, to have had the fecret of becoming
a fecond good Fortune to her Husband, to
have made him meet her often, two or
three hours after Midnight, upon affigna-
tions, to have rais'd in him the higheft
tranfports which a moft paffionate Lover
is capable of: And, in fine, by that means,
to have brought him one of the fineft Children in the World. Tell me, is not that
an argument of it ? That's extreamly plea-

B 2   fant

fant, (anfwer'd the Marchionefs) but pray, Sir, oblige me in explaining your felf. Madam *de Valoury* (reply'd the Chevalier) lov'd her Husband infinitely, whilft he had nothing but an averfion for her, fo far that he cou'd not endure her company, but won'd have a feparate Bed, which was a moft fenfible afflicttion to fo tender, fo fond a Wife. As fhe was one day endeavouring to guefs at what cou'd be the caufe of his behaviour, it came into her thoughts that it muft needs be the love of fome other, and, in a little time, fhe difcover'd that he was much taken up with a young Widow who was her Neighbour; fhe made an acquaintance with her, and manag'd her with fo much Wit and Addrefs, that in a little time fhe became her moft intimate Friend. This Widow was at Law with her Husband's Relations for her own Jointure, and her Childrens Fortune; fhe was none of the richeft, and the extraordinary expence of her Law-Suit ftreightned her very much. Madam *de Valoury* made ufe of this occafion, fhe folicited the Judges for her, lent her Money; and, in fine, did her fo many other fervices, that fhe engag'd her entirely to her Interefts; which was fo much the eafier for her to do, the Widow's heart being prepoffefs'd in favour of another.

her. That oblig'd her to make Madam *de Valoury* a confidence of the passion her Husband had for her, what discourse he had had with her, the Presents he wou'd have made her ; and, in fine, with how much spirit and vigour he continually press'd her. Madam *de Valoury* desir'd her not to refuse his Money, nor his Presents, proffering to deliver the Merchandise for her ; and thus, by confederacy, they manag'd the Affair. The Widow receiv'd his Presents, and pretended to yield ; but that which seem'd the most difficult, as she said to *Valoury*, was to contrive a place for the rendezvous, because she was much observ'd by those about her ; that her Woman never left her all the day, whom she durst not trust ; that she had a little Daughter extreamly sharp, who observ'd all things very narrowly, and talk'd very much, and that between the two, she had a great deal of circumspection to keep, unless she wou'd ruine her self. *Valoury* seeing what difficulties there wou'd be in the day time, offer'd to come in the night, when they were all in Bed. He told her, she need only give him the Key that open'd all the Doors, and there being but one Hall to go through, to come to her, in which no body lay, he cou'd be there without being seen, or making any noise ; and that

he

he wou'd be gone before day. The Widow told him, that her Woman, and her little Daughter, lay in a Closet within her Chamber, and that therefore he must not speak, nor make the least noise. She gave him the Key, and he did not fail of keeping the assignation. Madam *de Valoury* supply'd the Widows place, who had retired to another Room. Our Gallant came, and laid himself very softly down by his Wife, without being perceiv'd by any body in the House; she did not speak, and it was too dark for him to see her, so that it was no hard matter for her to pass for the Widow, in a place where he cou'd not imagine any other Woman wou'd be. Never Man was more charm'd with his good Fortune, nor in greater ecstasies of Pleasure! In fine, the poor Lady was afraid her Husband's Life, or at least his Health, was in danger. Day approaching he went away, and continu'd this little Commerce for some time; but the pleasantest part of the Adventure was, the Conversations he had in the day time with the Widow, expressing the dear Raptures of the Night, which he exaggerated to such a heighth, that she cou'd not refrain from laughing excessively. The better to divert her self with it, she ask'd him, coldly, the difference of those he tasted with
his

iis Wife. With my Wife! (reply'd he)
never have any, 'tis but by Duty, or
rather by neceffity, I ever converfe with
her; and if I had not need of her to raife
ny Money, (which I can't do without her)
fhou'd never fubmit to it. Her Flefh
(continued he) is loofe, her Skin rough,
fhe has no Neck, no moifture, her Lips
are cold and icy; can any thing be more
naufeous? We muft own, (faid Madam *de
Seligny*) lifting her hands and eyes to
Heaven, that there are ftrange unaccoun-
table things in Love! *Valoury* has an averfion for his Wife when he knows her;
her flefh is loofe, her skin rough, fhe has no
Neck, no moifture, and her Lips are without fire: And yet, when he takes her for
another, fhe has none of thofe faults, and
he has all the tendernefs and paffion for her
imaginable. But whence comes this?
(continued fhe) who can give me a good
reafon for it? He took her (reply'd the
Chevalier) for another than his Wife;
change of Diet whets the Appetite. That
argument is not juft (return'd Madam *de
Seligny*) fince 'tis the fame object he finds
fometimes difagreeable and diftaftful, and
fometimes agreeable and charming. May
be it is (reply'd *Berly*) that the Pleafures
of Marry'd People being permitted, they
don't fo lively affect the Senfes; Laws

B 5   and

and Prohibitions, make all Enjoyments the
more relishing. And I remember a wild
Expression upon this Subject, which I have
often heard in *Italy*, to exaggerate the most
sensible Pleasure, *Quale gusto si fosse pecca-
to.* Neither have you reason'd justly,
(reply'd the Marchioness;) Madam de*Valoury*
loves her Husband passionately, which, according to you, she wou'd not do, since
'tis no Sin in her to love him. I see (continued she) the true reason is that which I
gave you just now, which is, That Love
expires as soon as it is without agitation.
Valoury had nothing to wish from his Wife,
she was all his, he dispos'd as he pleas'd
of her Person, and her Heart ; and that is
it which stifles Love. For his Mistress, he
went to her but at certain hours in the
Night ; no doubt there was danger in it,
he had often fears, and apprehensions,
which nourish'd his Love, and redoubled
his Transports, and inclination for his
Wife, when he thought her his Mistress.
This puts me in mind (continued she) of a
Lady of my acquaintance, who is above
forty years old, and yet her Husband is
as fond of her as he was the first day
he Marry'd her. And in this manner she
preserves him so : She is in a continual
reservedness with him, haughty, and never suffers any familiarity ; her Bed is

part, and if her Husband wou'd pass Night with her, she puts on an affected iness, and anger, makes him buy her vours, and give her every time a twel.

I am rich I am

g. C

The End of the First Part.

THE
SECOND PART.

Whilst Madam *de Seligny* was talking thus, a Lacquey came to let her know, that the Baronnefs of *Chardonnay*, and the Countefs of *Reall*, with the Vifcount *du Pin*, and the Commander of *Fuiffez*, was come to wait upon her. Ah! Gentlemen, (cry'd the Marchionefs) what Pleafure are you going to have, in hearing this company talk upon the Subject of your Converfation! Thefe two Ladies, befides that they are as beautiful as any in *Paris*, they have Wit like Angels. As fhe fpoke thus the Company came in, and after the firft Civilities, when they were all feated, the Abbot *Sophin*, taking up the difcourfe, faid to them, You are come very opportunely, Ladies, to decide a difficulty which is between *Philocrates* and *Alcander*, about Marriage : *Philocrates* maintains, That there is much more fatis-
faction

fachion, and lefs uneafinefs, in the Life of
a married Man, than of one who is not fo;
and *Alcander* is of a contrary Sentiment.
What think you of it, Ladies ? (interrupted the Marchionefs.) That depends
upon the choice of the Perfon (reply'd the
Baronnefs of *Chardonnay*.) 'Tis almoft
impoffible (anfwer'd *Alcander*) to choofe
well, in a time when a Woman difguifes her
felf, and appears quite contrary to what
fhe is, or what fhe will be; whether that
be done by a natural temper, or by diffi-
mulation, ohe does not fuffer the lefs by it.
Whatever pains a Woman takes, (continued the Baronnefs) fhe can't diffemble fo
well, as not to be difcover'd by the clear-
fight. d. Well, Madam, (faid *Alcander*)
what quality do you require in a Woman
to make a good Wife? That fhe be, (reply'd the Baronnefs) Difcreet, Devout,
have Wit, and love her Husband. I have
feen fome (return'd *Alcander*) who had the
Character in the World of poffeffing all
thofe qualities, and yet their Husbands
were not the more happy: What chagrin,
what conftraint, has not a Husband to fur-
fer from a Wife who paffes for Difcreet?
She is prefumptuous, proud, full of her
felf; her Husband does nothing well; at
every moment fhe oppofes his Sentiments
and his Conduct; fhe will difcourfe of all.

rule all, and imagines that, (becaufe fhe
does not live in the Irregularity of other
Women) her Husband ought to have the
laft Obligations to her for a Vertue, to
which her Vanity is alone indebted. Nor
will the Husband of a religious Wife have
a better Bargain; fhe'll let her felf be govern'd by interefted Perfons, of falfe Judgments, who will diftract her Brain, mif-
manage her Actions, furnifh her Alcove
with Deaths-heads, make her drefs her felf
in an antick and fingular manner; and
who, under a pretence of Devotion, will
engage her to make her Family faft, almoft killing her Husband, Children, and
Domefticks with Hunger, and by her
Whimfeys and Chagrins make a Hell of
her Houfe. A witty Wife is no lefs to be
fear'd; fhe is infolent, opinionate, and ill-
natur'd; fhe defpifes her Husband, looks
upon him as an ignorant; nothing is well
thought, but what fhe imagines; and, inftead of minding her Domeftick Affairs,
fhe thinks of nothing but filling up ends
of Rhimes, making Verfes, and feeking e-
very month a good Place in the *Mercure
Galant*. Tho' the Wife, who loves her
Husband, feems to be the beft Lot, fhe is
not the leaft incommode, nor the leaft
burthen: as foon as the Husband is arriv'd
at a certain Point, he has no more Paffion,

o more Tenderness for his Wife ; mean
rhile when his Wife loves him, she soon
perceives his indifference ; that creates
ealousie, and night and day he hears no-
hing but reproaches ; to hear her speak,
e is Perfidious, a Traytor , a Villain ;
low innocent soever his Actions are, she
nterprets them criminally, and, upon the
sightest suspicions, writes to a Husband,
or a Gallant, that his Wife, or his Mistress
betrays him ; if her Husband laughs, or
rallies with her, or caresses her, that's,
says she, to conceal some new Treachery :
If he is thoughtful or chagrin, 'tis for being with her, or his impatience to be with
his Mistress. You have heard of her, who
upon a suspicion that a magnificent Suit of
Cloaths which her Husband had made ,
was to please a Lady who had a Suit of
Ribbands of the same Colour, threw the
Cloaths in the Fire before her Husband
rise : Of another, who, disguis'd like a
Footman, follow'd her Husband every
where, to discover his Intrigues ; and of
that other, who, transported with her Jealousie, met her Husband's Mistress upon
the high way, and, to give him a horror
and disgust for her Person, made her be
shamefully abused by her Moor, and her o-
ther Footmen, and treated like an infa-
mous Prostitute : Own, after this that a

Man who is thus belov'd by his Wife has
not a little to endure. You take all your
Characters in their Extreams (reply'd
Philocrates) a Woman may be difcreet and
devout, without being chagrin and troublefome ; witty, without being fantaftick
and proud ; and may love her Husband,
without being jealous. There are few
Women (reply'd *Alcander*) who can keep
the golden *Medium* ; all they do is in excefs. For my part (faid the Commander
of *Fuiffez*) if I were to chufe a Wife,
fhe fhould be handfome, witty and gay ; I
would have her love all manner of Pleafure, Gaming, Balls, Walks, Plays, and
Treats ; in a word, that fhe fhou'd think
of nothing but diverting her felf. You
reafon like a Soldier, (anfwer'd *Alcander*)
that is, one of a Profeffion for changing
Wives ; but a Husband has not that advantage after fix months enjoyment of his
handfome Wife, this witty, gay Wife,
when he has feen her rifing from her Bed,
with yellow Complexion, pale Lips, hea-
vy Eyes, diforder'd Head cloaths, and
has heard her talk in her negligent hours,
when fhe does not obferve her felf, or is
out of humour, adieu Tendernefs and Refpect, adieu Efteem ; he takes his Purfe
from her, refufes her what Money fhe
would have for her Cloaths, her Orna-

...ents, and for Play ; he repines at her,
...mplains, won't bed with her ; she soon
...rceives the change : It must be reveng'd,
...ys she, Necklace, Rings, Crochet, Jew-
...s, all is dispos'd of to get Money ; that
...es not suffice, a separation must be made,
...'s an extravagant unthrift, cries she, to
...e Judges, he keeps Mistresses in Town,
...ad has attempted against my Life ; in
...he, Suppositions, Lyes, Artifices, all is
... season for her : In this Interval the offi-
...ous Lover proffers his assistance, she ac-
...cpts it : He, like the Husband, is tir'd of
...er, despises her, and leaves her : She takes
...nother, and then another ; and strowing
...hus her Favours from Gallant to Gallant,
...e quickly loses her Honour and Reputa-
...ion in the World : Her Husband knows
...ll this, but dares not complain of it in
...ustice ; he can get no Witnesses, and her
...are Accusation will suffice to cast him,
...nd make him be condemned to a Restitu-
...ion of his Wife's Portion, which she has
...onsum'd the best part of. Judge, after
...his, if it be advantageous to marry a hand-
...me Wife. Well then, marry her foo-
...sh and ugly, (return'd the Commander.)
...shou'd not love (reply'd *Alexander*.) to
...lush in Company at the Folly and Imper-
...inence of my Wife. And for ugly (answe-
...ned the Chevalier) I don't advise him,
the

she must paint, and that's a vast Expence to
a Man. You appear very difficult and
cautious (interrupted the Countess of
Reall, addressing her self to *Alcander*) but
'tis such as you that are the soonest en-
snar'd; and to give my Sentiments upon
the Matter, 'tis more honourable and advantageous for a Man to marry, than to
renounce it all his life : Yes (pursu'd she)
after having seen the life and end of *Singa-*
mis and *Agamis*, I shall always be of that
Opinion. All the Company, who were
divided upon *Philocrates* and *Alcander*'s Dispute, had a Curiosity to know their Story, and begg'd the Countess to give them
a recital of it ; which she did in these
Words.

The *History* of Singamis *and* Agamis.

Singamis and *Agamis* were two Brothers,
born of an illustrious Family, and had
both very considerable Fortunes : My Mother was the dearest Friend their Mother
had in the World ; who in dying commanded them to be govern'd by her ; they o-
bey'd her so well at first, that they did
nothing of consequence without communi-
cating it to her. When they were arriv'd
to an Age which they might think of Marriage, my Mother spoke to them of it :

Her

Her Advice was, that they should both marry; Religion, and the fine Estates they had, serv'd her for a Reason; but neither of them would hearken to it: *A. gamis*, who was the eldest, had an invincible repugnancy to it, which she could not surmount; but for *Singamis*, tho' he seem'd very averse to it, yet she reduc'd him, and undertook to provide him a suitable Match; and in this manner she design'd it; she would have her of some Fortune, but did not stand for a little more, or a little less; above all things she requir'd, that she should be one born of a discreet and vertuous Mother, who had given her a good Education, perswaded that the Daughter would have the same Inclinations; she was so prepossest with that Belief, and had observ'd it so often, that when she heard of the Loosness or Gallantry of any young Woman, she never fail'd of raising her dead Mother, to show that the Daughter had done nothing but by her Example: She did not desire an extraordinary Beauty, saying, that its consequences were dangerous; and provided that a Woman had a gentile Air, and nothing shocking in her Face or Shape, she cou'd bear with the rest; because, said she, how destitute soever a Woman is of Beauty, if she have Modesty and Discretion, she always

ways

ways pleafes: She believ'd the *je ne fçav,
quoy.* Then (interrupted the Vifcount *a,
Pin.*) It was very neceffary to interrup;
me, (reply'd the Countefs of *Real* briskly :)
I declare if you do it again, I fhall think
my Story Fatigues, and will break it off:
Yes, Monfieur the *Vifcount*, (continu'd fhe
fmiling, and returning from her fharpnefs)
fhe was fo far perfwaded, that we feel
for one another a certain *je ne fçay quoy,*
of Love or Hate, that before fhe could determine in her choice of *Sophronia*, (in
whom fhe found all the Qualities fhe look'd
for to form a prudent Wife,) fhe would
know whether the *je ne fçay quoy* was not
contrary to her Defigns ; and thus purfu'd
her Refolutions. One day, having contriv'd that *Singamis* and *Sophronia* fhould
meet at a publick Place without knowing
one another, and without having the leaft
knowledge of her Intentions ; fhe fet her
felf to railly *Sophronia*, to jear her very
fharply, and even to turn her into ridicule
'twas eafie to know in obferving *Singamis*,
what he would feel for *Sophronia* ; in that
moment the *je ne fçay quoy* appear'd. The
Youth fuffer'd more than fhe ; he did his
beft to defend her ; and in going out he
own'd fincerely to my Mother, that he had
been vex'd at her for ufing the poor young
Lady fo ill. My Mother, without difco-
vering

vering her felf, made him fome little reproaches for it ; and telling him, fhe had
nothing of agreeable in her, drew a confeffion from him, that fhe wou'd pleafe him
better than another; that was what my
Mother wifh'd; fhe made no longer a my-
ftery of her Defigns; and, after having given him a Reafon for all fhe had done, fhe
made him confent to marry *Sophronia*.
what is moft fingular and remarkable in
this Adventure, is, that tho' many young
People had taken *Sophronia*'s part againft
my Mother, fhe had no Acknowledgments,
and was only fenfible of what *Singamis* had
done for her : fo much, that fhe cou'd not
forbear boafting of it inceffantly, as my
Mother was afterwards informed ; nor
did fhe delay to conclude the Marriage.
Ah, *Alcander*, (cry'd the Countefs of *Reall* here,) how intirely will you alter your
Opinion, when you have feen the different
Conditions of thefe two Brothers in the
courfe of their Lives, and in their Deaths !
There was nothing but Sweetnefs, Satisfaction, Confolations, Peace of Confcience,
and Glory, for *Singamis*, nothing but Shame,
Scorn, Chagrin, Defpair , and Remorfe
for *Agamis*, as you are going to fee.
Sophronia was officious, humble, and
difcreet with her Husband ; and in her Family fhe kept a charming mildnefs, ming-
led with a little feverity, with which fhe

made her felf belov'd, and engag'd all that
belong'd to her to do their Duty, without
ever brawling or quarrelling; and if any
thing was out of order, with the juſteſt
Reaſons, handſomely inſpired, ſhe informed their Judgments, and brought them
firſt to condemn their own Errors themſelves; it was not poſſible but ſo engaging
a Conduct muſt touch the heart of *Singamis*: But, in the mean time, his being married did not hinder him from having ſome
little remainder of his former Inclinations
either for Entertainments, Gaming, or his
old Miſtreſſes. *Singamis* lov'd to treat
his Friends; *Sophronia* receiv'd them in the
beſt manner in the World; ſhe had alwayſ
an open and ſmiling Countenance; ſaid a
hundred pretty things; and all things
were ſo well order'd at her Houſe, that
he was better pleas'd there than in any o-
ther Place. When *Singamis* return'd from
Play very late, ſhe wou'd open the Door
to him her ſelf, with an Air of Gaiety and
Kindneſs; and if he chid her for not being in Bed, ſhe anſwer'd him that her Servants had wak'd ſeveral nights before; and
that ſhe wou'd ſit up in her turn, that
they might be the better able to ſerve him
the next day; that ſhe cou'd ſleep in the
morning; and that, in fine, ſhe had a mind
to drink with him of the Liquor that was

o have ready againſt his coming home. If he obſerv'd in her Husband's Face any regret for his Loſſes at Play, without ſeeming to perceive it, ſhe wou'd ſpeak to him of People who were to bring him money very ſhortly, and always turn'd the ſtate of their Affairs on the beſt ſide: What ſhe had the moſt pain to diſgeſt, was his correſpondence with his former Miſtreſſes; however ſhe did not complain of it, nor how the leaſt diſcontent in her Face: but when ſhe had made any new Diſcovery upon it, ſhe wou'd retire into her Cloſet, to vent her Grief in Tears: If her Husband ſurpriz'd her in that condition, immediately wiping her Eyes, and concealing her Sadneſs, ſhe recover'd her former Looks, and liv'd evenly with him: if he prevented her, and unaccus'd, offer'd to juſtifie himſelf, ſhe receiv'd all he ſaid with a mild and ſubmiſſive Air, letting him underſtand that ſhe did not think her ſelf deſerving enough to poſſeſs him intirely, and that ſhe was not born for ſo great a Happineſs. Tho' ſo diſcreet and charming a Behaviour, as *Sophronia's*, was capable of withdrawing *Singamis* from all his youthful Extravagancies, a Son and Daughter which ſhe had by him, and to whom ſhe had given an extraordinary good Education, were no little helps to her;

Guittarr to perfection, and underſto
Heraldry, Geography, Chronology a
Hiſtory. Admire what Power a wiſe a
vertuous Wife, aſſiſted by amiable a
well educated Children, has over h
Husband's Mind, to bring him to h
Duty. This Man, who lov'd nothing b
Gaming, Feaſting, Women, and Drinkin
plays now no more but with his Childre
will eat no where but in his own Houſ
and can endure no other Company but h
Wife's. I can't (ſaid he often to m
Mother,) I can't enough admire my chang
I us'd all my Endeavours before I was ma
ry'd to cure my ſelf of my paſſion f
Play; I was inceſſantly in the Taver
and among Women, notwithſtanding t
many reproaches I made my ſelf for it, a
the remorſe I ſuffer'd; but now I have
great a horror and diſguſt for thoſe ſo
of things, that I cannot conceive what ſ
tisfaction I found in 'em then: My on
Pleaſure is in being with my Wife an
Children: I paſs my days the moſt agre
ably imaginable in ſeeing them play tog
ther and careſs one another; and all n
ambition is bounded in giving them a go
Education, and making them a conſider
ble Fortune. As the Counteſs of *Re*
ſpoke thus, the Baronneſs of *Chardonn*
interrupting her, ſaid, Madam, 'tis in
poſſible to be better pleas'd than we a

ith hearing yon ; and we are refolv'd
)t to leave you till you have finifhed your
elation, thô Play time. approaches, and
at we have engag'd our felves to be there
you know. I underftand you, reply'd
e Countefs ; you would have me make
end, I will obey you, Madam ; befides
lcander fuffers too much by the recital of
hat Pleafures Singamis enjoy'd in Marri-
e ; but let him not deceive himfelf, he
ll be yet wôrfe entertain'd with all I have
fay to him of Ayamis.

To conclude. (continu'd the Countefs)
gamis and Sophronia, having made it their
ole bufinefs and pleafure to form the
nds and Hearts of their Children, and
give them great Fortunes, they made
m the moft finifh'd Perfons, and the
ft defir'd Matches in Paris, and marry'd
m into the Families of fome of the chief
nifters of State ; which gave. them a
at elevation in the World, and being
occafion of making Singamis's Merit
wn, the King gave him a confiderable
ployment, in which he grew old with
nour, and dy'd with Firmnefs and Con-
cy in the Arms of his Wife, who foft-
his laft moments, by telling him, that
y cou'd not be faid to dye, who left
n Children as his behind them. After
Death, Sophronia difpos'd of what he

had left, and retir'd into a Convent, when
she dy'd with a lasting Fame of Sanctity.

You have seen, (pursu'd the Countess
the Life and Death of *Sineamis*, who marry'd by my Mother's Advice ; and I a
going to tell you, that of *Agamis* his Bro-
ther, who wou'd never hear of it ; afte
which you shall judge if I have not reaso
to advise for Marriage.

Agamis, young, handsome, rich,
quality, gallant, unmarried, and desig-
ing never to marry, did not fail of finding
those sort of lucky Adventures , aft
which young People run with so much
avidity ; however passing whole hours h
in a Closet, and sometimes in a Che
scarcely daring to breathe ; getting hal-
ly down upon Linen ty'd together, fro
a Chamber-window into the street, by t
Favour of the Night, and in fear of bei
surpriz'd by the Watch ; hearing, as
was retiring home, Musquet-balls abo
his Ears ; being attack'd by Assassinato
Ingratitude and Infidelity of Mistress
Doctors, Chyrurgeons, almost always
his Heels, were Inconveniences which d
hearten'd *Agamis* from aiming at these
imaginary good Fortunes, and made h
take the resolution of fixing himself to o
Person, with whom he fansied he might lo
agreeable Life. He cast his E

upon *Scortina*, who was a Maid under the
Conduct of a Mother, uneasie in her Fortune, and of a humour to suffer all things
for a good Entertainment, or the smallest
Profit : *Scortina* plaid her part to admira-
ion ; she was no great Beauty, but had
n her Air, and in her Carriage, I know
ot what of tender, and moving, which
harm'd, and with which she engag'd *A-*
amis very far. To have seen her, you
you'd have thought her the discreetest,
most reserv'd young Woman in *France*;
nd she had already deceiv'd many, who
ad look'd upon her as a Prize ; but *Aga-*
nis fell deeper in the snare than all the
est ; *Billets-doux*, Verses, Declarations of
Love, Plays, Opera's, Rings, Crochet of
Diamonds, Pearl-necklaces ; in fine, all
vays were try'd before he cou'd be heard ;
nd then he must believe, she yielded but
o the violent Passion she had for him.
One day as he importun'd her, (judge of
he Character of this cunning Creature,)
e threw her self at his Feet, protested
e had never lov'd any Man so much as
e lov'd him ; and bursting into Tears,
onjur'd him not to ruine her, in making
n ill use of the tenderness she had for him.
his Discourse stopp'd *Agamis*, who was
n Enemy to all Violence. You will love
e no more my Dear, (continu'd she) and

then arising triumphantly, she went and threw her self upon a Couch, from whence she look'd upon *Agamis* with insulting Eyes: The poor Youth has own'd to me since, that he was upon the Point of going to ask her Pardon, when she rowling her dying Eyes pretended to swound away: *Agamis* run to her assistance, and insensibly forgetting his Vertue, he gave himself up to the transport of his Love; not *Lucretia* ravish'd show'd such lively, or such ardent Sentiments of Grief and Vengeance; twenty times she leap'd to *Agamis*'s Sword, and as often offer'd to kill her self. Dissembling *Jilt!* 'twas only to give him the greater *Idea* of her: You imagine well enough, that having begun with this artifice, she made use of many others. To have judged by Appearances, she had an affection for *Agamis* beyond all that can be conceiv'd; upon the least disorder or chagrin he had, she was inconsolable; never Woman appear'd so disinterested; for him (she said) she wou'd have sacrific'd her Fortune, Life, and Honour; she had had a general aversion for all Men, and cou'd not conceive how she was capable of so violent a Passion for *Agamis*; mean while this was all meer cunning and dissimulation in which her Interest only was concern'd, and it was nothing for her to entertain two

or three Men at once ; but the poor cre-
dulous *Agamis* gave up his Faith entirely
to all ſhe ſaid, and believ'd himſelf the
happieſt of Men, in having found a Perſon
ſo ſenſible, ſo vertuous, and one who lov'd
him ſo tenderly ; which made him free
himſelf from all other Engagements, that
he might be wholly hers ; as ſoon as ſhe
perceiv'd it, ſhe begun with making her
ſelf Miſtreſs of his Houſe ; ſhe chang'd all
his Servants ; wou'd have the Purſe in pretence of good Huſwifery ; and influenc'd
him in ſuch a manner, as to make him
quarrel with his Relations, and break with
all his former Friends. In fine, all his Affairs were manag'd by *Scortina*'s Order:
She had a Son, upon which the wretched
Agamis madly doted, and thought of nothing but deceiving the Laws, to make him
Heir of all his Eſtate after his Death. *Scortina*, taking hold of that occaſion, prevail'd with him in a Sickneſs which he had,
to enter into many Obligations to her advantage, and ſome of her Gallants ; by
which he thought he cou'd hazard nothing,
having them in his poſſeſſion. To conclude, *Scortina*'s Son gave *Agamis* a thouſand diſturbances ; he wou'd be all the day
in Taverns and ill Houſes, and frequented
none but Robbers ; by and by they bring
him home drunk, and without ſenſe ; at

other times dangerously wounded; another day he muſt be hid, becauſe he has kill'd or wounded ſome body; and many times he was in Priſons, and upon the Point of receiving a ſhameſul and ignominious Sentence: In fine, his Brutality arriv'd to that heighth, that he offer'd ſeveral times to beat, and even kill both *Agamis* and *Scortina*: And, for her part, ſhe liv'd no better than her Son at laſt; but gave her ſelf to a thouſand Rogues, with whom ſhe drank, and committed a hundred other Infamies; which compleated the ruine of her Reputation and her Health: She communicated her Diſtemper to *Agamis*, who then began to know her, and wou'd have taken meaſures to get himſelf out of her hands; but ſhe perceiv'd it, upon which ſhe gave him a ſlow Poiſon; ſtole the Key of his Cabinet from him, and took his Money, and all the Obligations he had ſign'd in the time of his Sickneſs; retir'd from his Houſe, and by virtue of theſe Obligations made his Goods be ſeiz'd on, and deſpoil'd him of them all; ſo that the unhappy *Agamis*, abandon'd and deſpis'd by all the World, ſpoil'd and ruin'd by the Diſeaſe, and the Poiſon ſhe had given him, dy'd in extreme Miſery, and in the higheſt Deſperation.

The

The Countefs of *Reall* had no fooner ceafed to fpeak, than all the Company declar'd for Marriage, and was of *Philocrates*'s Opinion: The Marchionefs of *Seligny* declar'd her felf with more violence than the reft; fhe faid that a vertuous Wife has always certain Sentiments of Honour in her Heart, which gives incomparably more fatisfaction, than the irregular Manners of a Mifs; and that a legitimate Child finds in himfelf the Dignity of his Origin; whereas a natural Child expreffes, for the moft part, in his Actions, the fhame of his Birth, and the irregularity of his Parents corrupted Manners; and ended, faying with a fharp and raillying Tone, that one muft have a mind of a very uncommon and fantaftick Character, to defend a contrary Opinion. However *Alcander* ftill perfifted in his, and even maintain'd that they had never feen fuch Enormities committed by Miffes, or Baftards, as had been acted by Wives, and legitimate Children. Have we not known, faid he, a legitimate Daughter, harbour for three years, and put in execution the horrible Defign of poifoning her own Father, who lov'd her tenderly, and from whom fhe had receiv'd a thoufand Kindneffes? Was there ever any thing heard of to parallel that, done by a natural Child? Have not we lately feen a Wife,

who

who had given Money to have her Husband
be aſſaſſinated; another, who had rais'd
falſe accuſation againſt hers, which wou'd
have expos'd him to a moſt cruel and ignominious Death: Did ever ſuch things
enter into the Thoughts of a Miſtreſs, or
illegitimate Child; and yet they have been
acted by lawful Wives and Children, and
thoſe of Quality. They ſay Scortina poiſon'd Agamis, how probable is that? His
Death wou'd have made too great a noiſe
in the World; and ſo black an Action
cou'd not have eſcap'd the Rigours of la
Chambre ardente: It may be indeed ſhe
robb'd him; but how many Wives have
done as much, (continu'd he, looking with
a malicious ſmile upon the Marchioneſs of
Seligny,) upon which ſhe bluſh'd. The
Baroneſs perceiv'd it; and, fearing the
Converſation ſhou'd grow too hot, to prevent it, roſe haſtily; and, caſting her Eyes
upon her Watch, ſaid ſhe fear'd the Play
was begun, and that they muſt not loſe
time, but go thither immediately; which
ſhe did with all the Company, except Philocrates, Alcander, and the Abbot of Sophir,
who were more for walking. The Coach
was ſcarce out of St. Germains, when Alcander taking up the Diſcourſe, ſaid, what
ſhocking, extravagant Women are here?!
ow does that Baroneſs of Chardonnay

dare with an inch thick of red and white upon her face, to maintain that Air of Reservedness and Gravity? That confident Countess of *Reall*, ought not she to have dy'd with shame, in reciting such an imprudent Story as *Scortina*'s ; and for that Extravagance of *Seligny*, what think you of her, to rob her Husband, leave him, and sue him to a separation, because he loves her too well? How I pity (proceeded he) the unfortunate Men who are troubled with such Wives. Ah, how free is my *Lesbia* from those sort of defects? All the Women I see, serve only to make her appear the more agreeable to me ; pure Water is all her Paint ; but meeting a Man's Eyes makes her blush ; she keeps two thousand *Lowis'd'ores* for me, which I think safer with her than in my own Cabinet ; and is so disinterested, that I cou'd scarce oblige her to receive the Ruby which I gave her. All that *Lesbia* has done for you, (interrupted *Philocrates*,) comes not near the Obligations I have to *Frandelisa* ; she had broke off with *Philabell*, was resolv'd to leave the World, and confine her self to a Convent, but for me alone has chang'd her resolution, and me alone she loves.

As *Philocrates* spoke thus, the Sky had cover'd it self with a Cloud so thick and

dark

dark, that they cou'd hardly with the
help of the Lights diſtinguiſh their way,
which oblig'd their Coachman to drive as
faſt as he cou'd to the next Tavern. *Phi-*
locrates, *Alcander*, and the Abbot *Sophia*
being come out of the Coach, went into
the firſt Room in the Tavern, where they
found two Gentlemen who conteſted together about the Value and Beauty of a
Ruby ; he that had it in his hand, and
who was the Owner of it, ſaid, that it
was an Oriental Ruby, the other affirm'd
that it was not : *Alcander* calling to mind
that tho' the Ruby which he had giv'n
Lesbia was a very good one, many People
had taken it for falſe, had a Curioſity to
ſee that which the Gentlemen held , and
ſtepping ſoftly forward behind him, he
ſaw it very near ; it ſeem'd to him ex-
tremely to reſemble that he had preſented
Lesbia with, which cauſ'd ſome diſturbance in him : He who had the Ruby having turn'd his Head, and ſeen *Alcander* in
that condition, haſtily hid it ; and notwithſtanding the violent Rain, went preſently out of the Tavern accompany'd
with the Perſon with whom he was.

I wou'd fain know (ſaid *Alcander*) who
that Gentleman is to whom the Ruby be-
longs. I don't know him, (reply'd *Philo-*
crates ;) but for him that was with him,

can tell you his Name, (continu'd he ;) 'tis
Philabel, he that was desperately in love
with *Fraudelisa*, whom she cou'd not endure, and whose Visits she refus'd, because of his too free and disrespectful carriage. 'Tis the Owner of the Ruby (interrupted *Alçander*) that I would know ;
methinks his is very like that which I
gave to *Lesbia*, and I wou'd fain find out
from whence he had it. He is really jealous, (answer'd *Philocrates* , laughing,)
and thinks *Lesbia* gave his Ruby to that
Man. I am very far from it, (return'd *Alcander*,) I know *Lesbia* too well to do her
that Injustice ; the poor Creature was like
to dye for Grief when she lost it, and I
had much ado to comfort her.

Tho' *Alcander* was very confident of
Lesbia's Fidelity, yet the quick and con-
fus'd manner with which he had hid the
Ruby, the precipitation with which he
had gone out of the Tavern, tho' it rain'd
violently, and the resemblance he found
in his Ruby to that which he had giv'n
Lesbia, disquieted him, and gave him a
Chagrin; which was perceiv'd by the Abbot, and which oblig'd him to call one of
his Servants, and command him to inform
himself with addrefs,of the Names of those
two Gentlemen. The Fellow told him,
that apparently he shou'd not have much
difficulty

difficulty in learning them ; that they ha
fent a Footman back to the Tavern to fta
for the Anfwer of a Letter which was to b
brought thither ; that he was a Country
Fellow whom it wou'd be eafie to manag
with a Bottle.   One of the two, (faid *A*
cander to the Servant,) has a Ruby ;
thou canft learn from whom he had it, an
how, what Obligation fhall I have to thei
and how grateful fhall I be ?   The Servar
promis'd him to ufe all his Endeavours fo
his fatisfaction, and fo went out of th
room in order to it.

In the mean time, *Philocrates*, *Alcande*
and the Abbot, fell to making Reflection
upon what they had feen.   *Alcander* faid
that never any Ruby had more refembla
that which he had giv'n *Lesbia*, and th:
in feeing them together one might be de
ceiv'd. *Philocrates* alledg'd that moft R
bies were alike, and that it was very diff
cult to know their difference : The Abbe
did not know what to think of the furpri
and aftonifhment thefe two Men were i
and of their hafty retreat notwithftandi
the Rain.   *Philocrates*, with a difdainlı
and raillying Air, faid, *Philabell*, affecte
with his being to marry *Fraudelifa*, cou
not bear his fight, and therefore was r
tir'd : In fine, every one reafon'd after hı
fancy, till the Abbot's Servant came t
infor

Inform them, that the Owner of the Ruby was call'd *Cleanthus*; that a Lady had presented him with it, who was very shortly to give him two thousand *Lowis d'ore's*; and to be marry'd to him; that that Footman, (who belong'd to *Cleanthus*,) did not know the Lady's Name, but had only told him, that one day she and *Cleanthus* being in an Arbour in the Garden of St. *Clou*, and talking together, he had hid himself behind the Arbour, where he heard all that he told him.

After the Servant had giv'n this Account, and was retir'd, *Philocrates* casting his Eyes upon the pensive *Alcander*; 'Tis then thy *Lesbia*, (said he to him,) that Maid so mov'd with the loss of the Ruby thou had'st giv'n her: Alas! that Accident seem'd to her a presage that thou woud'st cease to love her; she believ'd 'twou'd be her death, poor Girl: Dost thou observe how disinterested she is, and how faithfully she keeps thy two thousand *Lowis d' Ore's?* That Maid so free from all Engagements, who hated for thy sake all other Men; that Heart which thou hast kept so well in breath, by the diversity of Exercise thou gav'st it, and by the fear of losing thee: In fine, that Heart which lov'd thee in a manner so nice, so delicate, and so unknown to marry'd People.

Don's

Don't insult over the unhappy, (reply'd *Alcander*;) In whom shou'd one confide! cry'd he; *Lesbia* give my Ruby to a Wretch, a Fellow without Name! *Lesbia* unfaithful to me! *Lesbia* treacherous! *Lesbia* resolv'd to rob me!

In whom shou'd one confide, (interrupted *Philocrates*,) in a Maid of Quality, well educated, and who looks upon you as her Husband; in fine, in *Fraudelisa*, in whom appears a thousand charming Qualities, a thousand Vertues? This Conversation was interrupted by the noise of a Footman, who had brought a Letter, and ask'd for *Philabell* in the Court.

Philocrates looking out of the Window, saw that it was *Fraudelisa's* Footman, which made him colour: *Alcander* observing it, had a mind to see who it was, and he knew him too; so that without giving any hint of his Suspicion, that perhaps he had brought the Answer, which *Cleanthus's* Footman waited for, he went immediately down; and having found in a passage, through which the Fellow must needs pass, a corner so dark that one cou'd hardly discern any body in it, he plac'd himself there to wait for him; and as soon as he was near enough, ask'd him softly for *Fraudelissa's* Letter, at the same time putting a Crown in his hand: The Footman,

who

who cou'd not fee him that fpoke to him
by reafon of the obfcurity, did not go to
imagine that it might be fome other than
Philabel, who ask'd for the Letter; and
not being very forry to have a Crown, he
took it haftily, gave the Letter without
making any farther reflection, and went
his way. *Alcander* as foon return'd to
the room where he had left his Friends;
and after having unfeal'd the Letter, he
gave it *Philocrates*, asking him if he knew
the hand; *Philocrates* anfwer'd that it
feem'd to be *Fraudelifa's*: And then *Alcander* told him how he got it; which you
may imagine gave both him and the Abbot
an extreme impatience to read it: And in
thefe Terms it was conceiv'd.

LETTER.

YOU are ignorant of what force the firft
Engagements have, and you as little
know my *Heart*, when you imagine it capable
of loving any Man but you; if I marry Philocrates, I fubmit to the cruel and terrible
Commands of a Father, who will facrifice me
to that great Law-fuit which has fo long de-
vour'd his Family. The Heart of the Victim
will not then be found of the Sacrifice; 'tis
deftin'd for a cruel, for thee, ungrateful Man.
Alcander

Alcander had no fooner read this Letter
then returning it to *Philocrates*, and look
ing upon him with a ferious Air, he fpok
to him in thefe Words: This Letter (fai
be to him) makes me change my Senti
ments, converts me from my Errors, an
reconciles me to Marriage. Ah, *Phila
crates*, (continu'd he,) how happy ar
you, that can for your whole Life engag
to your felf a Maid of fo much Honour,
one who loves you fo faithfully ! See how
fhe hates *Philabel*, that imprudent, un
mannerly Man, who made the poor Girl
blufh fo often ; how regular and agreea
ble a Life are you going to live together;
the more you fee her, the more you will
difcover her extraordinary Qualities, and
the more you will be fatisfy'd with your
choice; you will make of your Duty a
foft habitude of loving one another ; fhe
will furnifh you with a thoufand innocent
Pleafures, withdraw you from Debauche
ry, by an excefs of lawful Joys; fhe will
bring you the comfort of fine Children,
and the Letter fhe has wiit to *Philabel* af.
fures you of it. Here *Alcander*, quitting
his Gravity, cou'd not forbear laughing
heartily ; and, in that moment, the Coachman came in to advertife them, that the
Rain was over, but that there remain'd fo
thick a Cloud in the Air, that it feem'd
to

to threaten a more furious Storm than the
firſt; and that he cou'd not anſwer for
carrying them back, unleſs they ſet out
preſently; they order'd him to be ready.

The Abbot *Sophin*, ſeeing *Philocrates* and
Alcander, as it were out of themſelves,
ſpoke to them in this manner. You have
no cauſe to laugh, nor one, nor t'other,
and if any thing can diſengage you from
Women, it muſt be what you have now
ſeen; not that you ſhou'd judge of all by
Lesbia and *Fraudelisa*; there are ſtill ſome
Women of Honour and Fidelity. The
buſineſs is not (interrupted *Alcander*) to
diſengage us from Women, to condemn
or to commend 'em; we know enough of
them already: But now the Point is-to
judge between us, and to know if it is
advantageous to marry, and if there is in
Marriage more ſatisfaction than chagrin.
The Queſtion appears to me very difficult
to decide, (reply'd the Abbot;) but if
you will know what are the firſt Thoughts
that preſent themſelves to me upon the
Matter, I think that the Conſtitution
ought to be the only Rule in this difficulty: If you feel in your heart an indifference, or an averſion for a Wife, and for
Children, don't marry; for Marriage then
will certainly give you more chagrin than
pleaſure: If on the contrary, you find in

your self a difposition, and an inclination for 'em, you will do much better to marry; not that you are to hope for a real and a folid Happinefs, there is none in any Condition of this Life, and lefs in Marriage than in all others; but the lawful Pleafures of that State may ferve to foften the chagrin and pains of Life; to hinder your Wife from falling into Diforders and Debauchees, and to temper her ill humour and uneafinefs; you will receive Services from her; you'll have the pleafure of knowing your felf again in your Children; they will be as Bonds to unite you more ftrongly together, and you will find your Mind and Confcience in another Seat, than with a Miftrefs interefted and unfaithful. In a word, evil for evil, 'tis better to live with a Wife, who lets herfelf go but rarely, and that by weaknefs, to fome Infidelity, than to be all your days expos'd to the Perils, which your Fortune, Life, and Reputation hazards, with a Woman, who having no lawful tie for you, and being without Honour or Religion, is capable of undertaking all things, to fatisfie her Pleafure and her Paffion.

As *Alcander* was a going to anfwer, the Coachman came to them again, and oblig'd them for fear of a fecond Storm to take Coach, and return to their feveral Lodgings.

T H E

THE
THIRD PART.

IN the fame time that *Philocrates* maintain'd, tha.. there was more Satisfaction than Uneafinefs in Marriage ; that *Alcander* affirm'd the contrary ; and that
both entreated the Abbot *Sophin* to be
their Judge upon the Queftion, Whether
it was more advantageous to marry than
to live fingle : *Lesbia*, who had been *Fraudelisa*'s Friend ever fince they had been
Penfioners together in the fame Convent,
came to vifit her. 'Tis to wifh you (faid
fhe, running to embrace her) all Happinefs, a thoufand Pleafures in your Marriage. Yes, my Dear (return'd *Fraudelisa*,
preffing her in her Arms) I am going to be
the happieft Woman in the World, fince
I am to marry *Philoc ates*. I will believe
it (reply'd *Lesbia* with a ferious Tone,
feating her felf by her) but then your
Deftiny muft have fomething in it very
fingular, and *Philocrates* muft not be like
other Men. How many Women (purfu'd
the)

she) lament night and day their having ever engag'd in Marriage? Can that be possible my Dear (answer'd *Fraudelisa*)? 'Tis a dreadful thing (resum'd *Lesbia*) to subject one's self for ever to the Will and Infirmities of a Man, whom one knows but through an interested Gallantry, and an infinite number of Artifices and Disguises: he is no sooner become your Husband, than he looks upon himself as a Master, who has an absolute Empire over you, he neglects you, despises you, and think 'tis against his Gravity, and he does you a great Favour, when he receives your Caresses. I apprehend nothing on that side (returned *Fraudelisa*) *Philocrates* loves me with a Passion too tender and constant. You may find other Troubles in Marriage (continu'd *Lesbia*) as, the Evils and Accidents that attend, the Breeding, Bearing, and Lying-in of Children and the Afflictions that their Sickness causes, or their Death. Well (reply'd *Fraudelisa*) the Pleasure of bringing a Husband that one loves, a Child which he desires, recompences the Pain; if they are sick, there are Servants to take care of them, and if they die (pursu'd she Smiling) for one lost two gain'd. Do you reckon for nothing (assum'd *Lesbia*) the Cares, and Disquiets which is caus'd by the Desire

and Ambition of raiſing your Children,
and making them great, and the part
you take in the Fatigues and Troubles the
poor Husband endures, to make his Fortune, or to preſerve that which he has?
I ſhall know how to govern my Thoughts
(anſwer'd *Fraudeliſa*) to bound my Fortune, and my Ambition, and apply my
ſelf intirely to pleaſe my Husband, by my
Kindneſs, and good Humour; and with
us I need not fear wanting, we ſhall have
Eſtate enough, and our Parents have taken
care to ſettle it well. How many Men (reply'd *Lesbia*) have had greater Riches, and
high Employments, who are now in Neceſſity, or whoſe Widows and Children live in
Miſery and Servitude? but I'll allow (continu'd ſhe.) that your Family remain in
Honour and Opulency, who will aſſure you
that this Husband's Heart who is pleas'd
with himſelf, and ſeeks for every day new
Reliſhes of Joy and Pleaſure, ſhall always
love you, with that yellow Complexion,
thoſe pale and livid Lips, and that lean
Face which your many Children will without doubt bring you; whilſt he who goes
into the World, ſees Women every day,
as beautiful as Angels, who offer him
their Favours? As *Lesbia* ſpoke thus, the
Widow of a Merchant Jeweller came to ſee
Fraudeliſa, 'twas to ſell her a Pearl Necklace

lace. This Woman had let her have many Jewels at a very low rate, which occafion'd a great Intimacy betwixt them. See
(faid fhe to *Fraudelifa* turning the Necklace on all fides, and giving it to her) look
upon this delicate Drop, of what Bignefs
and Roundnefs it is. I'll warrant it right
Eaftern, or I'll have nothing for it; 'tis
to be fold for fix hundred *Lowis*; and if
the Lady whofe it is, and who has
made a falfe one like it to deceive her
Husband, had not play'd unfortunately
at *Baffet*, you fhou'd not have it at that
price. *Fraudelifa* told the Woman fh
wou'd fhew it to fome that underftood
fuch thing, and then give her an Anfwer.
Lesbia who knew this Woman, by having
feen her often at her Mothers, and having
bought fome Jewels of her, and knowing
that her Husband had not been long dead,
ask'd her if fhe was marry'd again. She
reply'd, That fhe was very far from it;
that there was no Condition fo happy as
that of a Widow; that fhe is indepen-
dant, lives as fhe pleafes, and is fafe from
thofe Reproaches which are ufually given
to Old Maids. You may change your
thoughts (return'd *Lesbia*.) I marry again
(Interrupted the Woman raifing her
Voice, and lifting up her Shoulders)
God keep me from it; I have had too

much of that already. Marriage was not made for such Wretches as I. Why so (anfwer'd *Lesbia*?) Men of our Rank (reply'd the Widow) look upon their Wives as their Servants, upon the firft Difquiet they fcold at them, call 'em a hundred Names, and if they anfwer, threaten to break their Heads; they muft have their Miftreffes in Town, but if the poor Wife entertain a little Intrigue, and they happen to perceive it, they rage like Devils, and are ready to kill her, as if that ought not to be reciprocal. It is not fo (continu'd fhe) with Women of Quality, their Husbands will fee nothing, and whatever prefents it felf to their eyes, they turn 'em from it, to prevent the Noife and Scandal. Let me tell you, Ladies, what my Fate was with my late Husband, and you fhall judge if I have reafon to think of Marrying again. I brought him a great deal of Houfhold-Goods, and Money, and at the beginning of our Marriage, one would have thought, by what he faid, he would always love me; I fhou'd be Miftrefs of all, and fhou'd never want any thing: but in a little time the Scene was changed, he became fo furly, and fo uneafie, that he cou'd not endure me; there was nothing but Grumbling and Quarreling perpetually; he car'd for nothing but

playing at Bowls, being in Taverns, and
with his Wenches, and never came home
but late at night, ſtinking of Wine and
Tobacco, furious as a Lion, ſwearing and
railing at me and his Children. If he was
ſick, I was forc'd to ſpend the whole days
and nights in ſerving him, and to ſell my
Merchandize at Under-Rates, for Money
to defray the Expences of his Sickneſs;
and for all my Recompence, he told me
I was a wicked Slut, that already wiſh'd
to ſee him bury'd. After his Death, the
Charge of the Funeral, and his Debts, have
conſum'd the beſt part of what I had, and
I have five Children left, and a Shop ill
ſtock'd, upon which my Induſtry muſt
maintain us. Judge now, fair *Lesbia*, if
I can ever deſire a ſecond Marriage. As
the Woman ſpoke thus, a Footman of
Alcander's ask'd for *Lesbia*, and deſir'd to
ſpeak with her in private. 'Twas one ſhe
had plac'd in his Service, that he might
give her an Account of all his Maſter did,
or ſaid, when he was from her. He told
her how the Rain had conſtrain'd *Philocrates*, *Alcander*, and the Abbot *Sophin*, to go
into a Tavern, where they had found *Cleanthus* and *Philabel* diſputing about the Value of a Ruby, which appertain'd to *Cleanthus*; in what manner *Alcander* had ſeen
the Ruby, that he thought it extreamly

refembled that which he had given her,
and how he had made *Cleanthus*'s Servant
be examin'd upon it: he added, that the
Foot-man had anfwer'd, that a young Lady, whofe Name he did not know, had
given it to his Mafter, and that fhe intended to prefent him with two thoufand
Lewis d'Ors more, and to be marry'd to
him; that *Alcander* had believ'd her to
be the Perfon of whom he fpoke, and was
fenfibly touch'd with it; and how *Philocrates* jeer'd him when he perceiv'd it. After this he related to her, that at the fame
time a Footman of *Fraudelifa*'s who had
brought a Letter, ask'd for *Philabel* in the
Court before the Tavern; that *Alcander*
(knowing from the Window where he was,
to whom the Footman belong'd) had fufpected a Commerce of Gallantry betwixt
Fraudelifa and *Philabel*, and to difcover it,
went to intercept the Letter; that he had
plac'd himfelf in fuch an obfcure Corner,
that it was impoffible to diftinguifh Perfons; where as foon as the Footman came,
Alcander ask'd him for *Frandelifa*'s Letter,
giving him a Crown, which he took, and
deliver'd the Letter; that *Alcander* open'd
it, and gave it to *Philocrates*, who knew
it to be *Fraudelifa*'s hand; and that he had
read it to *Alcander*, and the Abbot. This
Footman added, that he cou'd not remem-

ber the Words of the Letter, but that
he only knew the Sence to be, that she
marry'd *Philocrates* against her Will, to
obey her Father, and that she shou'd always love *Philabel*. He likewise told *Lesbia*, how *Alcander* had laugh'd in his turn
at *Philocrates*, for having been so confident
that *Fraudelisa* lov'd him alone; and in
fine, all that had been said by the Abbot
and them. And when *Lesbia* seem'd to
wonder how he shou'd know so much, he
told her, that he had hid himself in a Closet which join'd to the Room where they
were, from whence he had heard all.
When he had given *Lesbia* this Information, he left her, to return to his Master,
from whom he had stole away to seek
for her. This Relation affected *Lesbia* in
such a manner, and made so violent an
Impression upon her Face, that *Fraudelisa*
perceiv'd it, and askt her what was the
Cause of it? She reply'd, that it proceeded in part from the Concern she had
for her Interests; and *Fraudelisa* pressing
her to express her self more clearly, she
askt her if she had not writ that day to
Philabel, and what the Letter contain'd.
This Discourse gave an Alarm to *Fraudelisa's* Heart, which made her entreat *Lesbia* to tell her quickly all she knew of it:
Lesbia let her understand that she was un-
willing

willing to speak more plainly before the
Woman who was there : the Widow perceiving it, told her, that a Woman of
her Trade knew much of those Affairs ;
that she had learn'd a great deal in carrying Pearls and Diamonds to People of
Quality's Houses ; that they might confidently rely upon her Fidelity and Discretion ; that she had admirable Talents for
managing a Galantry ; that she found a
very great Pleasure in making Lovers happy ; and that if *Lesbia* wou'd speak bold-
ly, they should both see what a skilful
Person she was. *Lesbia*, who was as uneasie, and as much perplex'd as *Fraudelisa*,
was ravish'd to know the Widows Talent,
that she might make use of it in her Turn
if she found it as extraordinary as she promis'd: So that she continued telling *Fraudelisa*, that the Letter which she had writ
that day to *Philabel* had been intercepted,
and was in the hands of *Philocrates*, with
all the manner of that Accident. Immediately *Fraudelisa* call'd her Footman, and
askt him, to whom he had given her Letter: he answer'd (in a little Confusion)
that he had given it to *Philabel :* but *Lesbia* pressing him to tell her whether he was
certain that he had seen *Philabel*, he confess, that by reason of the Darkness of the
place where he was when he gave him the

Letter, he cou'd not diſcern his Face, but
that he was ſure 'twas *Philabel*, becauſe he
ſpoke firſt to him, and ask'd him for
Fraudeliſa's Letter.

Fraudeliſa having ſent away the Servant, chiding him, and being perſwaded
that undoubtedly *Philocrates* had her Letter, was ſo ſenſibly touch'd with it, that
ſhe fell down upon a Couch, and lay for
ſome time as immovable ; then coming to
her ſelf, ſhe ſpoke theſe Words, interrupted with many grievous Sighs : You
look upon me then, *Philocrates*, as an ingrate, as an unfaithful Woman, that would
have deceiv'd you with a falſe affected
Tenderneſs : Ah wretched *Fraudeliſa !* an
unhappy *Philocrates !* cry'd ſhe ; under
what unlucky Planet are we born ! Oh
that you cou'd one moment ſee the Sentiments of Eſteem and Love I have for you,
and thoſe of Hatred and Diſdain which I
have for *Philabel !* but no, I never can let
you ſee it, and I have now no Choice to
make but Death : What Conſolation ſhou'd
I find in that if I cou'd leave thee in thy
Heart an eternal Reproach for thy unjuſt
Opinion of me. But my Dear (interrupted *Leibia*) did you love *Philocrates*?
Did he love you? Ha! Did I love him?
return'd *Fraudeliſa* ; never was any Paſſion founded upon more Eſteem or Inclinatio

How modeſt, and reſpectful, was he !
what charming, ſoft, what paſſionate
things he ſaid to me ! he'll die with Grief
(unhappy Man) as well as I. Why then
(reply'd *Lesbia*) loving him ſo much as
you do, and being ſo well belov'd by him,
do you entertain a Commerce of Galantry
with *Philabel ?* 'Tis a long Story my Dear
(anſwer'd *Fraudeliſa*) which I am not in
a Condition to tell you. The Widow re-
preſented to her, that the thing was not
ſo deſperate as ſhe imagin'd ; that if they
knew her Story, they might give her ſome
profitable Counſel ; that we are blind in
our own Concerns, and more capable of
adviſing others than our ſelves : ſhe added, that ſince ſhe was belov'd by *Philocrates*, and did really love him, ſhe hop'd to
find ſome means to juſtifie her in his
Thoughts, and to reconcile them together.
This Diſcourſe a little ſettled *Fraudeliſa*,
and made her begin her Relation thus.

THE

THE
HISTORY
OF
FRAUDELISA.

AFter my Father and Mother had remov'd me from the Convent in which
you and I were, they took me home to
them, and gave me a Governeſs; but in
a little time it happen'd, that a great Law-
Suit in which they conteſted for the beſt
part of their Eſtate, was referr'd to the
Parliament of *Burgundy*; thither they
went, and left me with my Governeſs,
under the Conduct of an Aunt, who dy'd
preſently after their Departure; ſo that
my Governeſs had the ſole Management
of me. This Woman, inſtead of examining my Actions, to regulate them, applauded me in all, and was eternally
commending me, telling me, I was the
fineſt young Lady in *Paris*, and ſhou'd cer-

tainly make a World of Conquefts: this is very taking with young People, and it gain'd her a great Afcendant over me, which was all her Aim, as you will fee hereafter.

One day feeing me more gay, and more exact than ordinary in dreffing my felf, fhe took her time to tell me, that if my Beauty gave me Pleafure, it as much tormented a very fine Gentleman, who lov'd me with a moft violent Paffion; but fo fubmiffive, and refpectfull, that a Queen wou'd not be offended at it. I ask'd her his Name, but fhe conceal'd it; telling me, fhe wou'd let me guefs who he was. Upon the Walks the fame day, I faw a Man who never took his Eyes off me, but look'd on me with a paffionate Air, and fometimes our Eyes met. Ah, my Dear, what Deceivers Men are in thefe Moments of Surprife, he caft down his Eyes in a manner fo fubmifs, and fo full of Modefty, that I would have given him for a Pattern to the moft expert Novice in our Convent: Ah Cheat! Ah Traytor! 'twas only to enfnare me. Do you underftand that 'twas *Philabel* of whom I fpeak? by the Sequel you will fee how much my Governefs was at his Difpofal: She ask'd me after our walk, if I had found out my Lover; and I thought I had made a fine

Difcovery, when in defcribing him, fhe told me 'twas the fame fhe had fpoke of. He was a man according to her Character, that had not his equal for Noblenefs, for Courage, and for Merit; truly 'twas an Honour for me, that he wou'd make me a Vifit. How ridiculous one is when one does not know the World!. I receiv'd him very well, and was proud of my Conqueft. He gave me a pretty little Dog, and a young Parrot, that fpoke every thing: I pafs'd the days in kiffing and careffing the little Dog, the Parrot talk'd all night, and twenty times repeated, Ingrateful *Fraudelifa*, pity me; cruel *Fraudelifa*, pity the unhappy *Philabel*. He carry'd me to two Plays, to *Ariana* and *Andromache*. At *Ariana*, he wou'd willingly have fought with *Thefeus*, to punifh him for his fidelity. At *Andromache*, in certain paffionate and tender parts where *Pyrrhus* is ill us'd by her, preffing my Hand with Tears in his Eyes, he faid to me, that he was a thoufand times more unhappy than *Pyrrhus*, that *Andromache* had a Caufe to hate *Pyrrhus* fince he had been an Enemy to *Hector* her Husband; but that I hated him without having any reafon for it. I laugh'd at this Difcourfe, as who wou'd not have done in my place.

The

The next day I did not fee him, he was fick ; every day his Diftemper encreas'd he wou'd take no more Nourifhment, or Remedies and was refolv'd to die, as they told me. My charitable Governefs undertook to make me fenfible that I had committed a great Fault ; and that with fome Men of a tender Nature, there needed not fo much to be their Deaths. Immediately with Pen in hand, I make him Satisfaction ; I write two or three times to him, or rather I fend in my hand Copies of Letters which my illuftrious Governefs composed. I was in good earneft, and imagin'd 'twas to fave the life of a Man whom I believ'd I had fome Obligations to : the Letter fpoke of nothing but the violent Paffion I had for him, the eager Defire I had to give him fome Marks of it, and to do all things rather than fee him any longer fick. Was not I a very difcreet Girl ? Was not I finely governanted ? But you will judge better of it by the reft. The fick Man wou'd not mend, nor leave his Bed ; but I muft go to raife him ; which I did, tho' with Reluctancy : I had no particular Inclination for his Perfon ; he did not touch my Heart, the fight of him gave me neither Pleafure, nor Pain ; his Studyed, and affected behaviour did not pleafe me ; in fine, I lik'd nothing of him but

his

his Parrot and his little Dog. We found him in his Bed, decay'd and weak. They begun with telling us, that he had eat nothing in three days; then out of respect, as if I had been an able Physician, my Governess, and those who were in the Chamber with him, retir'd to another, and left me alone with my Patient, to talk with him in private of the State of his Sickness. The first thing he said to me was that he was resolv'd to die; that since I wou'd not love him, Life was but a burthen to him, and that he wish'd for nothing so much as to leave it. I confess to you, that I believ'd he spoke sincerely, and that I pity'd him; I called him back to life in the best manner I cou'd, and promis'd him, whatever he wou'd have, if he wou'd be careful of his Health, and eat something before me. Admire my Friend at my Simplicity; he eats part of a Chicken; I applaud my self for this great Cure, he gives me a thousand Thanks, and kisses my Arms a thousand times; which I took no care to hinder, for fear of a Relapse; my sottish Complaisance emboldned him. Ah insolence! Yes, against this sick, against this weak Man, I had occasion for my Teeth, my Nails, and all my Strength. Escap'd out of his hands, I made him a thousand outrageous Reproaches, charging him never to come any more into my Prefence; then I call'd my Governefs, who was very calmly in another Chamber; and went out of the Houfe with her, more furious than a Lyon: What, faid I to her, is *Philabel* then but an impudent Cheat, a villain, that has neither Tendernefs nor Refpect for me, and who defires nothing. but to triumph over my Weaknefs and my Honour! had not I been a pretty Creature, added I, if I had defended my felf worfe? durft I ever have appear'd in the World? and many other things I faid, too long to recite. All the time of this Difcourfe my good Governefs hearkned very patiently to me; and feeing me a little calmer fhe faid I fhou'd not alarm my felf, and that a lefs Beauty wou'd not have produc'd fuch great effects; that fhe knew very underftanding Women to whom the fame thing had happen'd, who never made any Noife of it; and that, tho' they had pretended an Anger and Refentment againft the Men, they efteem'd them the more for it in their Hearts; that I ought to do the fame, that the like Adventure had befallen to other Maids of Quality befides me, who had not come off as I did, and yet they were not lefs efteem'd in the World.

By this Difcourfe I preceiv'd all the wicked Defigns fhe had againft me, and her Intelligence with *Philabel* to ruine me : What Fury, what Indignation, did I conceive againft her! notwithftanding which, I muft diffemble, or lofe all.

As foon as I came home to my Lodging, I fhut my felf up alone in my Chamber, where reflecting upon the Softnefs, and tranquility of my Life, whilft I was in the Convent ; upon the Agitations and Difquiets, I had felt fince I came out of it ; the Deceits and Infidelities I had met with ; the fmall Duration of the Pleafures of this World ; the Shortnefs of Life, my Aunt's fudden Death, and upon a thoufand other fuch things, I took the Refolution of leaving the World, and becoming Religious, and I only waited for the Return of my Father and Mother, to put it in execution. *Mean while I liv'd in this manner*, the days I pafs'd entirely in reading the Lives of *Anchorets*, and Fathers of the Defart : charm'd with what I read, and in a ftrong Defire to imitate them, I had renounced all forts of Ornaments : I never went out, but to Church ; I had no Attach for any of the things of the World, and I tafted no other Pleafures but what my little Dog and Parrot gave me, nay even thofe I began to fcruple, when I confider'd

der'd from what hand I had them, and resolv'd to send them back to *Philabel*, which
I did. How my little Heart murmur'd
and suffer'd when I saw them carry'd
away ! I fansy'd there was Sadness in the
Eyes of the two poor little Animals as
they left me; and I needed all my Reason,
not to be overcome with Tenderness. The
Person who carry'd them had not been
gone a quarter of an Hour, when I saw
Philabel enter my Chamber, and throw
himself at my Feet, with a Complexion
pale and wan, his Eyes bathed in Tears,
Despair painted on his Face, and in a Condition so moving, and so pierc'd with
Grief, that no Heart cou'd be hard enough
to see him in it, without Emotion. He
said he was a perfidious Villain, a Brute,
unworthy to appear before me; that he
came to beg my Pardon, and to wash off
with his Blood the Injury and Offence he
had done me. In that moment he drew
his Sword, and was going to plunge it in
his Breast, if I had not withheld him: in
fine, I must or pardon him, or see him die.
I did it; because, said I, to forgive Injuries is a great Virtue : and as a Mark that
I forgave entirely, I was constrained to
retake the little Dog and Parrot ; which
was without much Violence, you may imagine. I let him know my Resolution of
leaving

leaving the World, and becoming Religious; I incited him to imitate me: he did
what he cou'd to put me off my Defign;
but finding me fix'd, he told me he would
take the fame, fince without me the World
would be burthenfome and infupportable
to him. In fine, we parted with moving
Adieus on both fides; I made him give
me a Promife not to vifit me any more,
fince his Prefence was an Enemy to my Intentions; and he drew another from me,
that in cafe I chang'd my Refolution, and
remain'd in the World, I wou'd love no
other than he, and be only his. My Refolution of being Religious appear'd to
me fo ftrong, that I believ'd I hazarded
nothing by that Promife; but you will
fee by the Sequel, that this Day's Mif-
fortune is occafion'd by that imprudent
Word.

I continu'd then to live in the manner
I defcrib'd to you before, not ftirring out,
feeing no body, always alone, never dreffing my felf, folely employ'd in Reading,
Meditating, and Praying in my Chamber,
which I had fo order'd, that it look'd like
a Hermit's Cell. One day when I was in
it, at my ufual Occupation, my Mother
who arriv'd from *Dijon*, with a Gentleman who led her, furpriz'd me there.
What Aftonifhment was there on both-

ídes! in me, for being found thus by her
ind that Man, at a time when I little expected her ; and in her, to fee me in that,
Condition : the poor ' ̮ ̮ ̮nan was fenfibly,
touch'd with it ; her firſt Thought was ̮
that my Aunt's Death had produc'd that
effect : ſhe threw her Arms about my neck,
and embrac'd me tenderly, without being
able to ſpeak ; and I burſt into Tears,
fcarce able to breath.   After theſe firſt
Movements, recollecting my felf, I fell
down at her feet, and embracing her knees,
begg'd her Permiſſion to go into a Convent, and become Religious.   She has no
Child but I, ſhe loves me extreamly, judge
of her Sentiments.   She did not declare
her felf, and without ſhewing any Repug-
nance to my Defigns, ſhe rais'd me up,
and keeping me in her Arms, ſhe told me,
that ſhe wou'd not oppoſe my Refolution,
if 'twas infpir'd by Heaven ; but that we
muſt firſt be fure of that, and not follow
every ſudden Motion ; that fometimes our
Youth , our Inconſtancy, or ſome ſhort-
liv'd Diſlike of the World, had the greateſt ſhare in them ; but that thoſe fort of
Engagements were of extraordinary confequence, being for our whole Lives, and
therefore ſhould be well confider'd.   She
added, that I was yet too young to have
a juſt Diſcernment of the World, or of

Religion ; that there was no haſte ; that
I ſhou'd dreſs my ſelf as became a Maid
of my Age and Quality, and not make my
ſelf remarkable by ſuch Singularity ; that
if hereafter I continu'd in the ſame
Thoughts , ſhe wou'd conſent to their
Execution, with all the Facility ſhe cou'd :
ſhe preſented that Perſon who came with
her to me, telling me, he was our Family's beſt Friend, and very capable of
giving me good Advice ; then ſhe retir'd
with him, and left me alone in my Chamber, where I made many Reflections upon
all that had befall'n, and all that had been
ſaid to me.

But, my dear *Lesbia*, I muſt make an
end ; I find I ſhall let my ſelf go to a Recital, that will not leave me in a Capacity of
profiting by thoſe Advices which I expect
from your Freindſhip. In fine, the Perſon whom my Mother gave me for a Coun-
ſellor, was *Philocrates*. 'Twas againſt his
Father that we pleaded ; the Proceſs had
already coſt above a hundred thouſand
Crowns ; it concern'd the Legitimacy of
my Grandfather, and of two Succeſſions of
my Unkles, which is to ſay, that this Proceſs wou'd have ruin'd us, and never have
been ended ; By good fortune it was in
the hands of one of the ableſt and moſt
diſintereſted Counſellors of that Parliament ;

ment; this Judge conferr'd about it with both Parties, made them senfible that neither their Fortunes nor Lives, cou'd terminate it; and by a Goodnefs which is not common to Judges, who will only judge, he wou'd inform himfelf of the State of the Families, of the two Antagonifts; and underftanding that *Philocrates's* Father, one of the Parties, had no Son nor Heir but him, and that my Father, the other Party, had only one Daughter and Heirefs, and that our Age and Qualities were fuitable, he propos'd (to put an end to the whole Difference) a Marriage. betwixt *Philocrates* and me, which was agreed to : fo that having made himfelf abfolute Mafter of the Bufinefs, inftead of an Arreft, he gave us Articles of Marriage, containing a Tranfaction and Donation, to our Advantage, of all that had been contefted for, which was fign'd with Satisfaction on all fides. In fine; the Parties reconcil'd came to *Paris*, to conclude the Marriage, at that time when my Mother and *Philocrates* furpriz'd me, as I have told you ; but they did not think it fit to tell me this News till my Mind was in another Difpofition. *Philocrates* came often to fee me in my Chamber ; at firft I look'd upon him as a Friend to our Family, and one my Mother had given me for a Connfellor. Ha

Ha *Lesbia*! how hard is it not to follow the Counsels of a Man made like *Philo-crates*, when they have such an aim as his had! I know not if you ever saw him; he is the handsomest, and most agreeable Man in *Paris*; an air of Quality open and sincere; all his Behaviour Great, Genteel, and Charming; a delicate and engaging Wit; a Heart tender, passionate, and e-qually capable of receiving great Passions, as of giving them: I found it by Experi-ence afterwards; my Heart and Mind was fill'd with nothing but him, I slept not Night nor Day, and employ'd my self wholly in endeavouring to discover his Sentiments for me: If he miss'd seeing me one Day, or came later, or went away sooner than usual, it gave me some Alarms. I persisted still in my Religious Designs, not so much out of a distaste for the World, as for the improbability I thought there was of my ever being *Philocrates*'s. I was utterly ignorant of his Sentiments, at certain times I fansy'd he had a disposition to wish me well; at others, that he laugh'd at my Weaknesses and me; at others, that as a Friend to the Family he only serv'd my Mother, and endeavour'd to bring me to her Desires. One Day that he was more pensive than usual, and that I quarrel'd at him for it,

he difcover'd to me what I fo much
wifh'd to know ; and holding one of my
Hands prefs'd in his, with a more tender and more paffionate tranfport than ordinary, he confefs'd to me, that I was
engag'd to him by Articles of Marriage :
He beg'd my pardon for having done it
without my confent, and for having conceal'd it from me, told me, in what
manner things were agreed on ; and
how by that our procefs had been finifh'd ;
then he fwore to me, that never Man
had lov'd fo well as he lov'd me ; that I
fhou'd be always Miftrefs of his Deftiny ;
that he had no defign to force my Inclinations ; and that he preferr'd the happinefs of pleafing me before that of being
my Husband. Never Daughter was more
refign'd to her Parents Will, than I appear'd ; I told him, that I was not forry
that Heaven had made choice of me to
be an Inftrument of finifhing a Procefs
fo pernicious to both our Families, and
that I would never bring any obftacle to
it. Ha! *Lesbia*, what obliging reproaches
did he make me in that Moment ! he faid,
I had only Sentiments of efteem and acknowledgment for him ; I was not
touch'd with his Paffion ; I acted but by
Confideration ; and in fine, after the manner with which he lov'd me, if my Heart
did

did not change, he shou'd not become the more happy by marrying me. This Conversation was interrupted by my Mother, who came into my Room, and found us both much discompos'd. *Philocrates* retir'd out of respect, and left us together: Then I gave my Mother an account of our Discourse, and what *Philocrates* had told me, which she confirm'd, and let me know, that if I desir'd to please her, I shou'd not deferr marrying him. I express'd a great deal of respect and submission to her Will, upon which she went away very well satisfied, and left me alone in my Chamber. 'Tis here, my dearest *Lesbia*, that I am not able to express the condition in which I found my self that moment: I form'd Idea's of imaginary Pleasures, representing to my self the advantage of putting an end to such a Process; the Glory and the happiness of being *Philocrates's* Wife, his Generosity in resigning all other Claims, and desiring only to obtain me from my self; his Submission in making me absolute Mistriss of his Destinies; the *delicateness* of his Sentiments, in wishing rather to be lov'd by me, than to become my Husband. Yes, yes, it is impossible to conceive the transports of Joy and Satisfaction which I felt; but Heaven always sells us very dear the Pleasures of this World,

and above all to me, who am the moſt
unhappy Maid alive, as you are going to
fee. At that very time, *Philabel*, who
had heard of *Philocrates*'s *Attachment* for
me, and that he was upon the point of
marrying me, guided by Fury and Deſpair, writ me a Letter, by which he
beg'd me to remember, the Promiſe I had
made him of never being any other Man's
but his ; and threaten'd, if I did not, to
ſhew my Letters to *Philocrates*, to pub-
liſh them in the World, and to ruine my
Reputation ; not thinking himſelf oblig'd
to obſerve any Fidelity to a Perſon who
had firſt broke her Faith with him. Ha!
what a fall from Happineſs at the reading of this Letter ! what Sadneſs ! what
Diſquiets ! what thou'd I do ; I fanſy'd
I already ſaw my Letters-running through
the World, and in the hands of *Philocrates*.
How ſhou'd I prevent ſo fatal a Blow, to
whom ſhou'd I have recourſe ? I found
there was a neceſſity of addreſſing my
ſelf to my Governeſs, by reaſon of the
intimacy that was betwixt her and *Philabel :* You have committed (ſaid ſhe to
me) a very great fault in promiſing *Philabel*, not to marry any Man but him ;
and to juſtifie your ſelf, you muſt pretend to him, that you love him, that you
have no affection for *Philocrates* ; that you

only marry him in obedience to the Commands of a severe Father, and that you shall not be the less his. I did so by the Letter that I writ to Day, which is fall'n into the hands of *Philocrates*, and which renders me the most unhappy Person in the World unless you take pity of me, and assist me with your Counsels.

Fraudelisa having ceas'd to speak, the Widow reassur'd her, and told her, 'twou'd not be so difficult as she imagin'd, for her to bring her self off; that she must arm her self with Resolution, and confidently affirm to *Philocrates*, that she was never capable of writing such Letters. How can I do that, (reply'd *Fraudelisa*) since he knows my Hand, and has many of my Letters, which it will be easie for him to confront with this last, and to confute me? The Widow pray'd her to follow her Fancy, and let her self be guided; and ask'd her, if she had ever a Copy of the same Letter, she told her she had, and presently took it out of her Cabinet, then the Woman made her write it over upon just such Paper as that which she had sent, with the same Pen, and the same Ink: The Letter finish'd, she told *Fraudelisa*, that she wou'd have it imitated by a Man, who was so admirable at Counterfeiting Hands, that there was

one but thofe who were very skilful,
hat won'd not be deceiv'd: After which
t wou'd not be difficult to impofe upon
Philocrates, if fhe play'd her part with
he leaft addrefs; that when he came to
eproach her with her Infidelity, and for
proof againft her, fhou'd fhow her the
true Letter, fhe muft be fure to take it,
and under pretence of going to the Window to examine the Character by the full
Light, turn her felf dexteroufly on one
fide, and when he could not fee her
Hands, flip the true Letter into her Pocket,
and fubftitute the Counterfeit in its
place; then return to *Philocrates*, give
him the Counterfeit, firmly maintain-
ing, that fhe did not write the Letter, and exprefs a great deal of Anger and Indignation at this procedure.
This Widow added, that if there ftill remain'd fome Doubts and Sufpicions in
Philocrates, he wou'd undoubtedly conferr
upon it with fome that were expert in
thofe things, who wou'd affure him that
the Letter was falfe, and not hers, that
then he cou'd think no otherwife, than
that it was a Trick of *Philabel*'s to hinder
him from marrying her; and that if *Philabel* fhou'd afterwards fhow her other
Letters, they wou'd by this become fufpected to *Philocrates*, and oblige him to

haften his Marriage, to come and beg her Pardon, make her a Confidence of all that had paft, and render his firft Efteem and Tendernefs.

This Widow had no fooner made an end, than *Fraudelifa*, apprehending with pleafure the Defign, and relifhing her Counfel, gave her a thoufand Thanks and promis'd to make her a Prefent.

Lesbia who was no lefs embarrafs'd than *Fraudelifa*, being pleas'd with the Widow's Advice, was very defirous to make ufe of it in her turn; and after having told her, that fhe was engag'd in a more troublefome Affair than *Fraude-lifa*'s, fhe intreated her affiftance in advifing her, and then inform'd her, that fhe was belov'd by *Alcander*, that he had promis'd to marry her, that fhe had a Contract writ, and fign'd with his Blood, that now he refus'd to perform it; that out of refentment againft him, fhe had refolv'd to abandon him, to take with her Two thoufand *Louis d' Or's*, to repair, in part, the Injury his breach of Promife had done her, and to go with *Cleanthus*, who had lov'd her a long time, and wou'd marry her; that fhe had prefented him with a Ruby which *Alcander* had given her; that to hinder *Alcander* from fufpecting any thing, and to perfwade him that it had drop'd from the Ring, and was loft, fhe had given *Cleanthes* only the Ruby, and had kept the Ring, but that unhappily *Alcander* had been inform'd of part of what had pafs'd; and that her concern was to know, how fhe fhou'd efface all thofe ill impreffions which he had taken of her Conduct, and regain his Confidence and his Heart. Our Widow reprefented to her, that what fhe had told them was not circumftantial enough, and that fhe muft give her a more particular relation of all that had paft, if fhe ex-pected any benefit by her Advice; to which *Frandelifa* added, that after the fincere manner with which fhe had related her Life, *Lesbia* could have no reafon to con-real any thing from them; which engag'd her to fpeak in this manner.

The End of the Third Part.

THE
FOURTH PART.

The History of LESBIA.

MY Father had spent all his Estate, and part of my Mother's Jointure, in the King's Service, and just when he expected a recompence from the Court, was unhappily kill'd at the Battle of *Senef*. My Mother, for the management of her Fortune, retir'd into a Religious House, to live there without Expence, upon a moderate Pension, and put me into that Convent, where our Acquaintance first began. 'Twas there, if ever, I tasted any sweetness in Life ; the Religious who had the charge of our Education, took a particular Inclination for me, and had no greater pleasure than having me shut up in her Chamber, to give me Instructions, which her Heart dictated as much as her Wit. 'Twas to advertise me, (as if by a kind of Prophetick Knowledge of what

as to befal me) that Men were deceit-
l, and unfaithful Creatures, in whom
ought not to confide ; that if I were
discreet and Vertuous, Providence wou'd
regard my Prayers, and take me into his
cotection ; that I shou'd be very careful
ot to fall into any Irregularity ; and in
afe I shou'd be so unhappy, she made me
mderstand, that I ought to come out of it
rith all diligence, if I would not draw
pon my self the scorn of the World, and
he Wrath of Heaven. I recite admi-
able Instructions to you, my dear *Fran-
elisa*, but you will see hereafter how
uuch I needed them. The tranquility
nd repose which my Mother and I enjoy'd
ras interrupted by a cruel Misfortune
rhich oblig'd us to leave our Solitude :
was to go and solicit a Process before the
arliament at *Rouen*, in which all we had
n the World was at stake. At our Ar-
ival in that City, we made an Acquain-
ance with an old Gentleman nam'd *Cleon*,
rho was esteem'd of worth and quality.
That which at first surpriz'd us, was the
assion and Zeal with which he acted in
ur Affair ; but when we learn'd that our
dve sary had just gain'd a Suit at Law
gainst him, we judg'd that Revenge had
t least as great a share in what he did for
is, as his concern for our Interests what-

ever it was, we receiv'd great Services by it
.One Day as we were very Gay, as
every Body flatter'd us with a happy Suc
cess in our Affairs, *Cleon* brought his Ne
phew *Cleanthus* to see us, out of pure Ci
vility, as he told us : Ah! what pass'd i
my Heart at that first sight! and what i
that of *Cleanthus* ! we blush'd, grew pale
and were so mov'd, and so out of ou
selves, that 'twas not possible for us to
speak a word to one another. There are
Hearts made for each other. The Vanity
Impudence, and Artifice of Men, their
mean endeavours to please, to appear
Beauish, Agreeable and Witty; their De-
baucheries, and the Documents of my
Religious, had given me such a disgust
for them, that I cou'd not endure them;
But I was not the same for *Cleanthus* : I
found none of those faults in him ; he appear'd to me Humble, Modest, Sincere, his
Wit natural, and without affectation; in
fine, I observ'd as much Prudence and
Vertue in all his Actions, as I saw Li
centiousness and Irregularity in those o
others. But admire this Conformity of
Inclinations : *Cleanthus* cou'd not endure
Women, for the same Reasons, and the
same Faults that I hated Men; which made
us conceive a violent Affection for one another. It was not oppos'd either by his

Unkle, who look'd upon him as his only
Heir, or by my Mother, their Defign being to marry us together, after we had
gain'd our Procefs. Ah, that unlucky Procefs which we look'd upon as gain'd, this
was its Deftiny. Our Adverfary brought
in a Paper very late the Night before the
Tryal; I think our Attorney call'd that a
new Production: and the next Morning
early it was try'd, and we caft, by that
curft Paper deliver'd in the Evening; and
what was yet more fevere upon us, was,
that my Mother was condemn'd to pay all
the Charges, which amounted to a confiderable Sum.

You may imagine how fenfibly my Mother and I refented this Lofs, if you remember that 'twas our whole Fortune we
contended for. That which augmented
my Grief, was, the unhappy State in which
I fanfy'd I fhou'd fee Cleanthus; yes, he
alone concern'd me more than all the reft
together; and I thought of nothing but
confoling him. But I did not yet know all
my Misfortunes, I faw Cleanthus no more;
I fent often to his Lodgings, and my Mother to Cleon's; but the Doors were fo
well kept, that we endeavour'd in vain to
get in; fo that we could not fee them.
My Mother began to miftruft Cleon; our
Caufe thus loft which he had warranted

F 2   that

the Gain of, and his Care to shun us, wer
her Reasons. At first I justify'd them bot
to her, prepossess'd with a Belief that ther
was some Misunderstanding: but after ha
ving a long time flatter'd my self, I con
cluded that *Cleanthus* had only lov'd me for
his Interest, and that the Loss of our Pro
cess, which left me without Fortune, wa
the Cause of his Behaviour and his Change
I conceiv'd at that time so great a Disdain
and Indignation against *Cleanthus*, that
took a Resolution, not only of never see
ing him in my Life, but ever not to stay
any longer in a City where there was so
great a Villain. I propos'd to my Mother
to leave *Rouen*, and go to *Paris*, to get
Counsel: she consented to it, and we set
out in our Coach, our Minds fill'd with
all that had befall'n us, and in a profound
Chagrin.

We had scarce rid an hour or two, when
a Stag of prodigious Greatness coming out
of a Castle, met our Horses, who growing wild and unruly, taking the Bit in
their Teeth, without keeping the Road,
they run into the middle of the Country,
over-turn'd the Coach, and drew us so for
some time. By good fortune, the Lady
of the Castle, who came out of it, seeing
our Mischance came to our Relief, with
many of her Servants, and brought us out
of

of that Danger. She found my Mother
wounded in many places in her Head; for
me, I was in a Swoon, and there was only some Scratches with Bryars and Thorns
upon my Neck and my Arms. They put
my Mother in one Chamber, and me in another; and I being still in a Swoon, they
undrest me, and put me to Bed. They
sent the Footmen all about to fetch Doctors and Chirurgeons, and left me one
moment alone in the Chamber. In that
same instant the Lady of the Castle's Son,
who return'd from Hunting, and who had
not heard of our Accident, came into the
Chamber where I was laid, and found me
in that Condition. After he was recover'd
from his first Surprize, he took me by the
Hand, and felt my Pulse. Just then I
wak'd out of my Swoon; imagine what
an Amazement and Fright I was in, to see
my Neck and Arms nak'd, and one of my
Hands in that of a Young-Man, whom I
had never seen before; and to find my self
in a Bed, and a Chamber, which I did not
know; I who thought my self in a coach.
I confess, I doubted for some time whether I was awake, or if it was a Dream;
but at last coming to my self, I took my
Hand from him who held it, and cover'd
my self all over with the Bed-cloaths. The
Gentleman was as much amaz'd as I, till his

E 4   Mo-

Mother, coming into the Chamber, clear'd
the matter, and inform'd us how we happened to find our selves in that manner.
This Man was *Alcander* ; who begun from
that time to love me, and to persecute me
with a Passion, which renders me the most
unhappy Wretch alive. My Mother and
I being perfectly recover'd, we thank'd
our Benefactors, took Leave of them,
and pursu'd the Road to *Paris*. We had
not travell'd a League, when we saw *Alcander* Galloping towards us ; 'twas to
proffer us, by his Mother's order, an
Apartment in a great House which she had
at *Paris*. We accepted his Offer, he
came into our Coach, sent back his Horses,
and conducted us. I never saw a Man
more Solicitous to please ; he turn'd his
Wit to a pretty Pleasantry ; had little
Stories upon all Occasions ; and Songs,
with a Voice sweet and clear ; he talk'd of
nothing but the Tenderness of his Heart,
and the *Delicateness* of his Sentiments : In
fine, I perceiv'd he had a mind to make
himself be lov'd ; *a d'autre a d'autre*, said I
to my self ; *Cleanthus* has taught me too
well what Men are, ever to look upon
them again but with Disdain.

The Journey ended without any further
Explication ; *Alcander* lodg'd us in magnificent Apartments ; I had a Chamber
adorn'd

adorn'd with curious Italian Pictures; he
eft us at reft for fome time, and we
faw him very rarely. Shortly after, we
learn'd that our Antagonifts had rated
the Expences, and bragg'd that they woo'd
feize our Goods and imprifon my Mother;
which made us pafs our Nights and Days
in imploring the Juftice of Heaven, and
in Tears. But I was more firm and refo-
lute than my Mother; I faid to her that
Providence was juft; that we had never by
our Actions deferv'd, Shame, or Infamy,
and that having Recourfe to, and Relying
upon his Goodnefs, he wou'd not abandon
us, but would bring us out of this unhappy State, and upon the Faith I had in
what my Relegieufe had faid to me, I fpoke
with fo much affurance, and fo perfwa-
fively, that I comforted my Mother, and
made her leave her Melancholy and her
Fears. One day (judge of my furprize)
being alone in my Chamber, I faw Alcander come in, who throwing himfelf at
my feet with Tears in his Eyes, conjur'd
me to pity the unhappy Condition to
wlich I had reduc'd him; and told me,
that after the Death of his Wife he had
made a Rofolution never to marry again;
that it cou'd not maintain it felf againft me,
fo amiable I appear'd to him; and that in
fine he muft either fee me his wife, or I

E 5   muft

muſt ſee his Death. I confeſs to you
that I had ſome Joy at this News; not ſo
much for *Alcander*'s Quality, and Fortune,
as becauſe that *Cleanthus* hearing of this
Marriage, would conceive the greater value
for me, reproach himſelf with his Ingratitude, and be griev'd for having loſt me.
However, I referr'd *Alcander* to my Mother, without giving him any Anſwer. He
ſpoke to her of it; ſhe wou'd have his
Mother's Conſent: he told her, that ſhe
intended to have him marry a Daughter of
one of her Friends, which wou'd make her
againſt it; that by temporizing he might
gain her Conſent, or ſhe might die, being
very old, and always Sick. My Mother,
who at the expence of her Life wou'd have
marry'd me advantageouſly, entertain'd his
Propoſals, and inſinuated to me, that con-
ſidering my Circumſtances, I ought not
to loſe that Occaſion. I follow'd her Counſel, hearkning calmly to whatever he wou'd
ſay to me; in concluſion, his Intention
was to marry me ſecretly: we cou'd not
get a Prieſt who wou'd do it; he told
me, that the Conſent of the Perſons only
made a Marriage; he gave me a promiſe
of marrying me ſign'd with his Blood,
brought me to the foot of the Altar,
ſwore that he took me for his Wife; I
made the Vow on my ſide too: Behold him
the happieſt of Mortals; but his happineſs

was interrupted when he offer'd to make
bfe of the Privilege of Husbands ; I re-
puls'd him, us'd him ill, was enrag'd at
him ; Quarrels between us, Reconcile-
ments : Reafons on his part to eſtabliſh
his right of Husband, and to put himſelf
in poſſeſſion of it ; Inflexibility on mine :
Tears, Defpair, refufing to Eat, refolving
to Die ; that was what I had my mind fa-
tigue'd, and my ears ftun'd with, at every
Moment ; however, I perfifted ſtill, in refolving firſt to have all the forms. At this
time my Mother's Antagoniſt had made a
Command be giv'n her, of paying the Charges : the next Day, for want of Money,
fhe was to be put in Prifon, and her Goods
feiz'd. It feem'd to me, that this News did
not touch *Alcander* enough : I complain'd
of it to him ; he made me Anfwer, that if
I wou'd own him for my Husband, and live
with him as a Wife, he ſhou'd have the
Sentiments of a Son-in-law for my Mother,
wou'd acknowledge her in that Quality,
and find out the means to aſſiſt her in her
Bufinefs ; that I ſhou'd confult my felf upon it ; that he ſhou'd fee on this Occafion
if I had any Nature, that he wou'd return in a little time to receive my Anfwer,
and went away thus. Ha ! when I faw my
felf in this defperate Condition, how many
different Thoughts had I, how many feveral

ral Movements did I feel! on one hand
I represented to my self my Mother shamefully dragg'd into Prison, and all her Goods
seiz'd by my permission, and with my Consent: on the other hand, I saw that our intended Marriage cou'd not justifie my
yielding to *Alcander*, what he ask'd, and
that if I did, I shou'd lose all I had of most
valuable, and fall into an Abyss of Misery
and Infamy. I call'd to mind then how
often I had heard my *Religieuse* say, That
Heaven is acknowledging of what is done
for him; that he does not refuse a discreet
and vertuous Maid what she Implores of
him; and, that he takes her under his Protection; which comforted me, and determin'd me to confide in that. On another
side, the Refusal which that Providence
had made me of the gaining our Process
so just and so reasonable, and which I had
beg'd with such ardent Prayers, with the
unhappy Condition in which we were,
and which I thought we had so little merited, gave me a Distrust of that same Providence; so that I wou'd not abandon my
self intirely to his happy Care. In this
restless and unhappy State, I cast my eyes
upon some of the Pictures in my Chamber
a fatal Curiosity mov'd me to draw a
Curtain which hid one of them, 'twas a
naked Piece, representing *Venus*, in the

Arms

Arms of *Mars*, and their sporting at the
time when *Vulcan* made them be surpriz'd
by the Gods. What Charms! what Pleasures! what Beauties! struck my Sight!
I did not look upon them as Pictures; they
gave me the same Movements that real
and substantial Beauties wou'd have done.
In that instant I felt an Emotion, my heart
sigh'd with it, a Languishment ran through
all my Veins, it shook me with a soft horror, which till then was unknown to me:
Ha *Fraudelisa!* how unhappy are our Sex,
not to be able to defend themselves at certain moments, from those sort of Weaknesses! Unfortunately, in that fatal Moment, *Alcander* came into my Chamber
to know my Resolution: he perceiv'd the
Condition in which I was; he interpreted
it to his Advantage; he made use of it,
and prest me with so much Eagerness and
Spirit, that I lost all Knowledge, and
knew no longer what I did. I only remember that my Reason rais'd in my heart
Motions of Indignation and Anger against
Alcander; that afterwards the same Reason, surpriz'd and inchanted by my Senses, and in Conspiracy with them, to deceive me, represented to me, that I sav'd
a Mother from Prison, and that by it I engag'd a Husband to my self. In this unlucky, in this fatal minute, *Cleon*, who
ar-

arriv'd from *Rouen*, and was come to visit
my Mother and me, finding a Key in the
Lock of the Chamber where I was, with
Alcander, open'd the Door without knock-
ing, and enter'd suddenly: he was so ter-
ribly struck to see me in that manner, that
he got out hastily, shut the door again,
and went away: Ha! what did I not feel
when I came to think, that *Cleanthus* hearing of my Conduct, wou'd applaud himself for having abandon'd me! No, I shou'd
never have comforted my self, without
the Thought that he wou'd afterwards
krow of my Marriage with *Alcander*. To
solace my *Chagrin*, and the more to assure
my self of him, I caress'd him, I call'd
him twenty times, my dear Husband, my
dear Heart, and begg'd him to think of
his Mother-in-law, and to bring her out
of this troublesome Business. *Alcander*
was no more so sensible of my Caresses, he
appear'd to me cold and indolent, and said,
that a *Minor*, as he was, cou'd not command Money; that my Mother had nothing to do, but to make a Sale of her
Goods, and to retire into a Convent. At
this Discourse I was much afflicted, I wept
and I complain'd of him; he went abrupt-
ly out of my Chamber, and left me; I run
after him; he flies before me. Just then
a Footman came and stopp'd me, to give

me a Letter which I knew to be from *Cleanthus* ; it imported, that he was at the heighth of Felicity, since he was short-ly to be my Husband ; that *Cleon* his Unkle was gone for *Paris*, to carry my Mother the Money to pay the Charges to which she had been condemn'd, and with a De-sign to bring me with her to *Rowen*, to con-clude our Marriage ; that the Reason why he had not seen us before our Departure, as to his particular, was because that the News of the Loss of our Cause had touch'd him in such a manner, that he fell sick up-on it ; that he had lost all Knowledge, and that the Physicians had charg'd his Ser-vants not to let any body see him : and as for his Unkle's part, that animated by the Concern he took in our Interests, he had secretly taken Post for *Calais*, where he had been to seek for a Paper that wou'd prove the Falseness of that which had oc-casion'd the Loss of our Suit ; that he had brought it ; and that it wou'd be no Diffi-culty to recall the Sentence which had been given against us, and to regain our Pro-cess. This poor Man, tho' he was not quite recover'd, did all he cou'd in his Letter to let me see how well he lov'd me, and how impatient he was to make me his.

Ha, with what a cruel Blow this Letter stabb'd my Heart ! What said I within my felf ! *Alcander* is inconftant, ingrateful, and unfaithful, and I have done all for him : thou lov'ft me ftill, unhappy *Cleanibus*, thou art faithful to me, and thou wilt marry me ; yet I abandon thee, I fhamefully betray thee ; thy Unkle comes to take my Mother from Prifon, thy Unkle wou'd have us marry : Tell me (continu'd I) can thefe Sentiments hold againft what he has feen ? and thou, canft thou refift againft what he fhall tell thee ? canft thou yet love me ? or rather, canft thou hinder thy felf from looking on me as the vileft Wretch, and hating me mortally ?

Tis I at prefent (purfu'd I) unfortunate Mother, that keeps thee Prifoner, and am the Caufe that thy Misfortunes fhall never end. Juft Heaven ! cry'd I fighing, I wou'd not wait for Succour from that favourable hand which was ready to help me ; I wou'd not truft to it ; and now I am miferable for the reft of my Life.

I thought and faid many things which it wou'd be difficult to recite to you. In conclufion, the violent Agitation of my mind, and the profound Sadnefs which I felt, made fo wonderful a Revolution upon my Senfes, that I fell dangeroufly fick. My Mother cou'd not overcome this laft Misfortune ; fhe had retir'd into a Monaftery, where fhe dy'd oppreft with Sorrows.

Con-

Courage, Courage, (said I) Fortune redouble thy Blows. I form'd to my self a kind of Pleasure, to see my self at the highest point of Adversity, believing they must now end with my Death: but my hour was not yet come; I was recall'd to Life or other Miseries.

Alcander put on Mourning a little after my Mother's Death; I imagin'd it was for his Mother-in-law, that is to say, that he look'd upon me as his Wife: I had not yet suffer'd enough for my Sins: now I was quite out of Danger; I know not if the secret Joy I had to see my self *Alcander*'s Wife, did not very much contribute to it. However, the impressions of the Distemper were too strong to be so soon cur'd: I did not sleep at all, and was extraordinary restless; three or four times a day an Apothecary's Boy brought me Syrups ready prepar'd, and Juleps. One day when the Curtains of my Bed were drawn close, and that I believ'd my self alone in my Chamber, my Mind being fill'd with nothing but *Cleanthus*, these Words chanced to escape me; Ah, unhappy *Cleanthus!* Just in that instant I saw the Curtains open, and the Apothecary's Boy that brought my Syrups throw himself upon his Knees by my Bed-side, saying to me with Eyes bath'd in Tears, and a Heart
full

full of bitter Sighs ; Yes, lovely *Leibia*, ye
he is more unhappy than you can conceiv
I cast my eyes upon the Boy ; but a Peri
wig which he wore, the Dress he was in
the Leanness and Decay which appear'd
his Face, embarrass'd me for some time
at last I knew him to be *Cleanthus* : w
were both so discompos'd, that we remain'
a long time unable to speak to one ano
ther, but by Looks and Sighs. He told
me, That his Unkle being return'd to *Rouen*
had spoke to him very disadvantageously
of me ; that he had said I was a Maid with
out Honour or Virtue, and had commanded him never to see me more, or think
of me : he added, That knowing me, and
the covetous, interested Temper of his
Unkle, far from being capable of thinking
such a thing, he had believ'd that his Unkle's Counsel at *Paris*, having judg'd our
Cause not to be good, and that we con'd
not regain it, he had contriv'd this Artifice
to give him a Disgust of me, and to hinder
him from marrying me, having had no o-
ther Prospect in our Marriage, but the
Gain of our Process, and to be reveng'd
of his Adversary. *Cleanthus* told me likewise, that in that Opinion he had made
some displeasing Reproaches to his Unkle,
for breaking his Word with us ; and had
said, that he was a Man of Honour, that
                                              be

he wou'd keep his Faith inviolably, and
have no Wife but me: that this Answer
had irritated his Unkle so much, that he
refus'd to see him, and that he had marry'd a young Woman, on whom he had
settled all his Estate : that tho' he had reason to be sensibly touch'd with such a Loss,
his Concern for not hearing from me had
made him forget that Misfortune, and determin'd him to come to *Paris*, to enquire
after me: that there he had heard of my
Indisposition, with a great deal of Grief,
and that not knowing how to see me otherwise, he had plac'd himself with the Apothecary who serv'd me, under pretence of
learning the Trade; that he found himself
well recompenc'd of this innocent Artifice,
since he had been so happy as to render me
some little Service in the time of my Sickness ; that he might now protest to me his
Passion (far from being lessen'd by Time
or the injust Reports that had been made
to him of me) was grown so violent, and
rais'd to such an Excess, that he con'd live
no longer without seeing me ; in fine, that
he came to learn his Destiny from my
Mouth, and that his Life was in my hands.

Who wou'd not have been mov'd, dear
Frandelisa, with a Proceeding so tender,
and so faithful? Indeed I was most sensibly;
but that did not hinder me from representing

ing to him, that tho' I shou'd think it my
greatest Happiness to see my self his, yet
we ought not to think of it; that we had
neither of us any Fortune; and that it was
indispensibly necessary in Marriage, if one
wou'd not make themselves miserable: I
confess to him, that I had believ'd him unfaithful, not hearing of him after the Loss
of our Process; that I had been extreamly
afflicted at it; and that a little time after,
my Mother had promis'd me to *Alcander*;
that because of his imagin'd Infidelity, I
had consented to it; that *Alcander* waited
only for the Death of his Mother (who
was very infirm) to marry me; and that
he had exprest his Sentiments, by having
put on Mourning for my Mother: He reply'd to me, with Tears in his Eyes, that
the Passion he had for me was so disinterested, and so wholly fix'd to my Interests,
that he wou'd willingly become a Galley-
slave to make me a Queen, for no other
Reward, than that I shou'd be pleas'd with
him in my Heart for it: but that I ought
to be perswaded, that *Alcander* wou'd not
marry me; that his Sentiments were too
far opposite to Marriage; that he only desir'd to deceive me; and that the Mourning he wore was for his own Mother, deceased a few days after mine.

As he spoke thus to me, we heard my

Nurſe upon the Stairs, who was comming
to me and talking with the Doctor;
which made *Cleanthus* riſe and leave me
haſtily, for fear of diſcovering ſomething
by the Trouble and Confuſion we were in.
The Conſolation I felt by ſeeing him, and
finding him tender, and faithful, work'd
ſuch a ſudden Effect upon my Senſes, and
Spirits that in a little time I ſaw my ſelf
recover'd; they ſlattered me that I grew
handſomer after my Sickneſs; and I believ'd it a little, when I ſaw *Alcander*'s
Paſſion for me much augmented: never ſo
much Aſſiduity, ſuch Complaiſance! his
only Care was to bring me the fineſt Ornaments, and Jewels and to give me all ſorts
of Diverſions; he wou'd have me keep
his Purſe; he had giv'n me two thouſand
Lowis d' Ors to keep; I was Miſtreſs of
all, he never call'd me otherwiſe than his
dear Wife. To conclude, I liv'd with him
as with a Husband, flatter'd with hopes,
that as ſoon as the Year of Mourning for
his Mother was out, he wou'd marry me
publickly, and own me to be his Wife:
but you cannot conceive what I ſuffer'd in
the time of that Expectation. Ah! how
different from others are thoſe Pleaſures
which are not lawful! and how wretched
is a Maid when ſhe is fall'n into that ſhame-
ful Extremity! She dares not appear in

the World; fhe thinks they fpeak of nothing but of her, and of her Infamy;
every thing makes her fear, nothing gives
her Confolation ; her Life paffes in Difquiets and continual Remorfes; her Lover
only loves in her his own Salacity and
Pleafure, without confidering whether he
pleafes or difpleafes ; fhe foon perceives
it : tho' fhe hates Tobacco, tho' fhe dreads
the Smell of Wine, tho' his wild and de-
bauch'd Behaviour, or his ill Humour, fatigues and torments her, he daigns not to
take notice of it; fhe muft fuffer, fhe muft
diffemble, and to preferve him, muft feign
Ecftafies and Ravifhments of Love and
Pleafure. A Wife makes a Vertue of thefe
fort of things for her Husband : the hono-
rable Figure fhe makes in the World, her
orderly Family, her fine Children, that in-
difpenfable neceffity of Living and Dying
with her Husband, their common Interefts,
the Satisfaction of doing her Duty, the
Repofe of Confcience ; all joyn'd together,
take off thofe fort of Diftafts, and furnifh-
es a marry'd Woman with new Pleafures,
which are unknown to one who does not
live within the Rules. For thefe Reafons,
I refolv'd to make *Alcander* declare himfelf as foon as the Year of Mourning was
over ; and in cafe he wou'd not marry me,
to abandon him, as a perfidious Traytor:

Cleanthis had left the Apothecary's
oufe; and after having often fought, in
in, Occafion to fpeak to me in private,
at laft found one: 'twas to tell me, that
Icander, in the Mind and Humour he was
, wou'd never marry me; that he came
offer me his Affiftance to be reveng'd of
m; that tho' the greateft Misfortune
hich cou'd befall him in the World, was
fee me in another's Arms, the Pleafure
f my Fortune, of my Elevation, and the
cknowledgment I wou'd have for him in
he depth of my heart, wou'd much affwage
s Grief. What Sighs, what Tears, did
is Converfation coft us! in fine, it ended
y a Promife which I made him; that in
fe *Alcander* (after the Year of Mourning
r his Mother) wou'd not marry me, I
ou'd be guided by his Advice. No, I can-
ot exprefs to you the diverfity of Move-
ents which appear'd in him that moment.
grows late, let us advance, my Dear.

The Year of Mourning for *Alcander's*
lother being ended, he wou'd not marry
e; and thefe were his fine Reafons: That
e were already marry'd, and might con-
nue and live in the fame manner with
afety of Confcience, fince Confent alone
ade a Marriage, which we had given one
other; that a publick Marriage, and in
f the forms, is not fo agreeable, nor fo.

voluptuous; that 'tis oppofite, and contrary to Love; that the Heart does not agree with it, it loves Liberty, and cannot act by Duty; and that as he defign'd to love me all his Life with the fame Fervour and Tendernefs, he wou'd not marry me otherwife. I anfwer'd on my fide, that 'twas to deceive our felves, to think our Marriage good, when our Religion and our Laws condemn'd it; that a Marriage after the Forms, was not attended with Contempt and Infamy; that it was without Fears, and without Remorfe; that one was not fhamefully oblig'd to hide the Fruits of it, but might behold them with Joy; that the Children, in whom their Parents have the Pleafure of finding one another, were Bonds which united them more ftrictly in Inclination and Interefts; that thefe Ties were much ftronger than thofe of a flitting Paffion; that a generous and well-difpos'd Heart found its Pleafure in its Duty, and form'd it felf to a foft habitude of following it: in fine I concluded that I faw very well he did not love me, fince he cou'd fee my Difquiet and my Shame, without being touch'd with it, and refus'd to fubmit to a Law which oblig'd him to love me all his Life.

This Refufal afflicted me the more fenfibly, when I found he had deceiv'd me by

his Promise writ and sign'd with his Blood,
which he cou'd release himself from, because of his Minority. 'Twas then that
reflected very seriously upon the little
Profit I had made of the Instructions my
Religieuse had given me: what Sorrow and
Repentance had I for it! I had not forgot
to have heard her say, That when a Maid
unhappily had fall'n into that Precipice,
She shou'd not lose the time of withdrawing
her self from it, unless she wou'd abandon
her self to the last Disgrace and Infamy:
That Thought made me take the Resolution of leaving *Alcander*, and marrying
Cleanthus: But oh, what sharp Reproaches
did I not make my self! what did I not
suffer when I came to think, that I had now
no more to bring into the Arms of a sincere
and faithful Lover, than the shameful Lea-
vings of a perfidious Traytor, and how
little I deserv'd *Cleanthus*'s Esteem! No,
tis impossible to express to you all that
pass'd in my sad Heart. In fine, I advertis'd *Cleanthus*, that I wou'd speak with
him; he came to the Rendezvous, and
here I inform'd him that *Alcander* wou'd
not marry me. Our last Resolution was,
that I should take my time to leave *Al-
ander*'s Lodgings, and to carry with me
the two thousand *Lowis d' Ores* which he
had given me to keep, with all I had of
my own, that de also Fig-

lowing the Advice which had been given me by a Lawyer, I shou'd retire into a Convent: that I should sue *Alcander* for the Performance of his Promise; and that after the Decree, which cou'd go no farther than to Interest and Damages, because of his Minority, *Cleanthus* should marry me. As a Pledge of my Faith, I took a Ring of Value which *Alcander* had given me, from my Finger, and gave it to *Cleanthus*; but both of us considering, that *Alcander* missing the Ring, might have some Suspicions of my Conduct, I took the Ruby out to give *Cleanthus*, and kept the Ring upon my Finger to shew *Alcander*, and to make him believe the Ruby was lost. That which made me most uneasie, was the Infidelity I was guilty of to *Alcander*, in violating the Trust he had repos'd in me of the *Louis d'ores*; but *Cleanthus* convinc'd me by so many good Reasons, that we are not oblig'd to keep our Faith with Villains and Traytors, that I yielded to his Perswasions.

Afterwards *Lesbia* recounted to *Frandelisa* and the Widow, that when she expected *Alcander* to go to a Hunting, by which he wou'd give her a favourable Opportunity of leaving him, and executing the Design she had form'd, he unhappily return'd that the same day the ill Weather had obliged him to go into a Room of an Inn i *bel* about the quality and price of the Ruby, which she had given him. and which *Alcander* had presented her with: that *Alcander* having advanc'd softly behind *Cleanthus*, whilst he had the Ruby in his hand, he had seen it, and thought it much resembled that which he had given her, and that *Cleanthus* perceiving it, in spight of the Rain had gone immediately out of the House,; that this Proceeding had given *Alcander* violent Suspicions against her; that to clear them, he had made a Footman of *Cleanthus* who stayed behind in the Tavern, be cunningly examin'd; that this Footman had answer'd, that a Lady whose name he did not know, had presented his Master with the Ruby, and that she was to give him two thousand *Lowis d'Ores*, and to marry him. In fine, she added, that *Alcander* had believ'd it to be her, of whom the Fellow spoke: and therefore she cou'd not doubt but that he was in a furious Rage against her: that she did not know how to retrieve his good Opinion, and make him believe it was some other Person of whom the Footman had told that Story; and concluding, she said to *Frankelisa*, and the Widow, that she shou'd have the last Obligations to them, if they cou'd give her any Counsel, and Means to recover this unlucky Step.

Lesbia having ended her Difcourfe
the Widow told her, fhe had reafon indeed to fay, that her Affair was more
troublefome and embarraffing than *Frande-*
lifa's ; and then after having Study'd a little, fhe ask'd her whether *Alcander* knew
her Story with *Cleanthus*, or at leaft to
her Knowledge: to which *Lesbia* anfwer'd,
that fhe had govern'd her felf fo well in
that, that not only he had not known
any thing of it, but that he belie'd fhe
had no Acquaintance with any Man but
himfelf. Can't you (continu'd the Widow) get the Ruby again which you
gave *Cleanthus*? Yes indeed. How, (interrupted *Frandelifa*) how, won'd you have
her to ask him to give her her Ruby again?
We muft buy another juft like it then reply'd the Woman, and *Alvarez* has them
of fo many Fafhions, that in his fhop we
fhall eafily find what we feek. Well (return'd *Frandelifa*) when *Lesbia* has fuch
a Ruby, what fhall fhe do with it; what
will be the Confequence? She fhall make
it be found in the Houfe, (anfwer'd the
Widow) by one of *Alcander's* Servants
who will carry it to him: *Alcander* (continu'd fhe) not knowing of your Acquaintance with *Cleanthus*, and not imagining
that you can have heard of what has paft,
that he faw *Cleanthus* have a Ruby, and

ſuſpected it to be that which he had given
you, will without doubt believe that he
was miſtaken, that it was not that which
he gave you, but ſome other, and that
the Account the Footman, gave, was of
ſome other Perſon than you; and between
our ſelves (concluded ſhe ſmiling) if you
play your part well, *Alcander* loving you,
you may perſwade him what you pleaſe;
for 'tis eaſy for a fair Lady to make a
Man who loves her, believe that ſhe is
faithful to him.

As the Widow ſpoke thus, *Lesbia*
thought upon a place that wou'd be convenient to make the Ruby be found in; ſo
returning a thouſand Thanks to her,
and to *Fraudeliſa*, ſhe told them, that ſhe
hop'd to make ſucceſsful Uſe of their
Advice: and it growing late, they went
preſently all three together out of *Fraude-*
liſa's Houſe, and firſt to the Copyiſt, to
make him imitate exactly *Fraudeliſa*'s
Letter to *Philabel*; and whilſt he was
buſie at that, they went to look for a Ruby
like that which *Alcander* had given *Lesbia*.
They found one perfectly reſembling it.
Lesbia bought it: then they came back to
the Copyiſt, who had imitated *Fraudeliſa*'s
Letter ſo well, that her ſelf was deceiv'd
in it; and after having embrac'd, and
kiſs'd one another, they parted, *Lesbia* and

F 2   *Fraudeliſa*

Frandelifa, going to difpofe all things for the next Day's Expedition.

Frandelifa folded up, and feal'd the Letter, in the fame manner as the true one was, then broke the feal, put it in a little Apron pocket which fhe had, and went to Bed, meditating all night how fhe fhou'd bring about her Defigns.

Lesbia on her fide, retir'd too, but took, at an Apothecary's by the way, a dofe of ftrong Phyfick; and being come home to her Lodging, having a Key to *Alcanders* Clofet, which fhe had made without his Knowledge, fhe put the Ruby which fhe had bought, in that place where he kept his Letters, hiding it under fome of them; becaufe that a few days before fhe had given the Ruby to *Cleanthus*, fhe had offer'd, whilft *Alcander* was by, to take from thence a Letter feal'd with filk, which fhe had a mind to fee, but he had hindred her, and fqueezing her fingers had forc'd her to lay it down in that place. *Lesbia* intending to make him think, that the Ruby had drop'd at that time, and fo continu'd there; then fhe lock'd the Clofet, and went to bed, her mind being folely employ'd on what fhe was to execute the day following.

The next day *Philocrates* rife earlier than ufual, impatient to exprefs himfelf

with

with *Fraudelisa*; he found her at her Toy-
let, in a part of the Room that was a let-
tle obscure; and seated himself by her
with a chagrin, and pensive air; she
feign'd to be surpriz'd with it, and ask'd
him the Cause. You shall see it, *ingrate*,
said he, in this Letter, giving her that
which she had writ to *Philabel*: she took
it, and then aproaching the Window, and
turning aside, she slipt it into her Apron-
pocket, and took from thence the Copy
which she had caus'd to be writ the night before; but so dexterously, that *Philocrates*
had not the least suspicion of it; then she
examin'd the Letter in his Presence with
a seeming Attention, and looking often
upon it, express'd a great deal of Surprise,
and Astonishment. See, faithless Creature,
(continu'd *Philocrates*) in what Stile you
writ to *Philabel*, that Man whom you called so impudent, so insolent, whom you
hated so much, and whom you told me
you had forbid to see you: he is worthy
of you (pursu'd he) and I will never be
an Obstacle to your Passion. Thats to say
(interrupted *Fraudelisa* sharply) that you
believe this Letter to be my hand, and
that I writ it to *Philabel*: you know but
ill (continu'd she with a cold, disdainful
Air) my Hand or my Heart; you that offer to tax me with Ingratitude, and Infidelity

delity. After this she writ the same Letter over before *Philocrates*, and having finish'd the Copy, she threw it to him with that which she had suppos'd, saying, Now see how you deceive your self, but don't think (pursu'd she haughtily) that I do this for any Pretension that I have to your Heart ; no, I renounce it all my Life, and what I have done now, is but for my own Satisfaction and Honour. Thus she left him, and went into her Mother's Chamber, without deigning to hear him speak. *Philocrates* took the two Copies of the Letter, examin'd, and confronted them ; one while he believes them both to be *Fraudelisa's* Hand, then again he thinks 'em different ; what shou'd he do ? to whom address himself ? to the Writing-Masters ; in their, Opinion the Letters are of different Hands, and *Fraudelisa's* innocent : the Abbot *Sophin* is not absolutely of the same Mind ; they dispute together, they consult, they wander in their reasonings, and know not what to determine certainly upon it.

As for *Lesbia*, as soon as Day appear'd, she secretly took the Physick which she had prepar'd and waited it's Effects ; when it begun to operate violently, she sent a Footman to tell *Alexander* from her, that she was dying, and desir'd to speak with him.

him. I dye with Willingness, said she to him, seeing him approach her Bed, and I have no Regrets for Life, since you are false to me, and that I cannot be your Wife. Then she feign'd a Convulsion Fit, the strength of the Physick, and the alteration it had made upon her Face, contributed much to hide her Deceit, and to perswade *Alcander* that she was really dying. After some time, pretending to recover from her Fit, she continu'd to speak thus: Hear me, *Alcander*, I have but little time to live, and my minutes are precious: Take, said she sighing, the Keys of my Trunk, the Money you gave me to keep, which is in it, and all I have of Value in the World; I give you all I have, and I wish I had a Scepter, and a Crown, to offer you in dying; after my Death, you'll see the Difference betwixt *Lesbia*'s Fidelity, and that of your other Mistresses; and I shall then be at the bottom of your Heart, to make you feel the Torments which are due to the perjur'd and unfaithful. *Alcander* was in a Surprise and Amazement, which cannot be conceiv'd, and his Resentment cou'd not hold against the Condition in which he saw *Lesbia*; nor against the Marks she made appear to him of Tenderness, and Love. He wou'd know the Cause from whence such sudden and extraordinary Effects cou'd proceed, and instantly begg'd of *Lesbia* to tell it him.

She begun (pretending to take new Forces) with telling him, that she had not slept all that Night; that when it was almost Day she had fall'n into a little Slumber, but had scarce tasted the first Sweetnesses of it, when a frightful monstrous Woman had appear'd to her, the very Remembrance of whom made her tremble still. She describ'd her to him, saying, she had hollow Cheeks, a wide Mouth, black and thick Lips, a flat Nose, large Nostrils, her Skin yellow, and mark'd with spots of Blood, her Eyes half out

of her Head, from which Fire inceſſantly ſparkled
her Head erect, and Serpents twiſted round it, inſtead
of Hair. She continu'd ſaying that ſhe ſeem'd to
her to diſappear a moment after, ſnatching a Serpent
from her Head which ſhe flung at her; that this Serpent ſlipping upon her hand, had faſtned on the ring
which Alcander gave her, and pull'd out the Ruby
with his Teeth ; then went and hid it in that place
where he laid his Letters, after which ſhe diſappear'd:
that at the ſame time abundance of Ravens, Owls,
and Bats, aſſembled upon her Head, in the form of
a Canopy, and made a fearful noiſe with their
Cries ; when a tall Woman, handſome, and with
an Air extreamly ſweet, carrying an Olive branch in
her hand, had chas'd them away ; and vaniſhing,
had thrown upon her Bed a Leaf of her Branch;
that ſhe wak'd immediately ſo perſwaded that ſhe
ſhou'd find the Olive-leaf, that ſhe had look'd a long
time for it ; and in fine, that ſhe had fall'n into ſuch
violent Convulſions, that ſhe plainly ſaw, ſhe ought
to think of nothing but dying : that theſe Ominous
Birds came to advertiſe her of it, and the weakneſs in
which ſhe found her ſelf made her ſee ſhe had but few
hours to live; after which, ſhe gave as the Laſt
Adieu's to Alcander intreating him to remember her
alſways, and to keep the Reſolution he had taken of
never marrying ; then without hearkening to what
he won'd, ſay, ſhe turn'd to t' other ſide ; begging
him to leave her the little time ſhe had, to think upon her ſelf.

Never Man beheld himſelf ſo much embarraſs'd as
Alcander was, he knew not what to do, nor what
to think : Solitude pleas'd him, he retir'd to his
Cloſet, he caſt his eyes upon his Letters, and ſeeing
ſome of them remov'd in that place where Lesbia
dream'd the Serpent hid the Ruby, he had the Curioſity (as he was laying them in their Order) to
ſearch

search the place: Ha! how was he surpriz'd when he found a Ruby there! he knew not who, or where he was, and fancy'd all he had seen was an Illusion. In this Condition he run to the Abbot Sophin's, where he found *Philocrates*, who told him, that the letter was not from *Fraudelisa*, that she was innocent that he had been convinc'd of it; and in general, all that he knew, upon that Subject.

Alcander on his side, recounted to them both, all that had pass'd in his Adventure; and after many Reflections, the Opinions of *Philocrates* and *Alcander* were, that *Lesbia* was innocent, as well as *Fraudelisa*; but the Abbot suspected some Artifice in it. That which amaz'd *Alcander* and *Philocrates* to the last degree, was *Lesbia's* Dream; nothing was so diverting, as the Explications they gave it, and the Stories, and Reflections they made upon the Significancy of Dreams: That great hideous Woman who flung the Serpents was *Discord*; the other, soft and beautiful, was the *Goddess of Peace*, who with her Olive branch, had chas'd the Ominous Birds away. They maintain'd to the Abbot *Sophin*, that there are Genius's and Spirits which advertise us in Dreams, of what is to befall us; and instanc'd in *Calphurnia's* which had foreshown the Death of her Husband *Julius Cæsar*; that of *Crœsus*, which told him his Son *Atys* shou'd be kill'd with a Dart, that of *Astyages* King of *Media*, which advertis'd him that the Son which shou'd be born of his Daughter *Mandana*, was to be Master of *Asia*. In fine, they told many more, and their Conversation ended with a Reflection they made, that one ought never to judge of any thing, since such strong and violent Presumptions as these were deceitful.

After all this Discourse, they told the Abbot *Sophin*, that they wou'd not leave him till he had decided their Question, whether it was most ad-

vantageous to marry, or to live without a Wife.
You determin'd (answer'd *Philocrates*) upon a false
Letter: you judg'd corrupted *Alcander*) upon
grounds which are not true; your Decision then may
be Erroneous: so that (added they both) we have
a Right to appeal from your first Sentence. That
which I have to give each of you (answer'd the Abbot) I had from one of the greatest Men in the Uni-
verse; I don't advise you to Marriage (said he addressing himself to *Alcander*) if you find in your
self a Vertue firm and constant enough to sanctifie
you in a perfect Continence: I don't forbid it you
continu'd he; turning to *Philocrates*) if you find it
necessary for the Good, and Repose of your Conscience; but know both of you, that for what concerns the Choice of that State of Life, as of all
others, we ought to look upon no other Consideration, and direct our Conduct but by that alone.

As *Philocrates* and *Alcander* were going to answer,
several Abbots of the first Quality came to visit the
Abbot *Sophia*, which oblig'd them to withdraw; the
Abbot waiting on them to the door, rally'd them
about their Mistresses, and taking leave, bid them
with a pleasant Tone, go quickly and reconcile themselves with them; and addressing to *Philocrates*, he
told him laughing, that he ought to rely upon what
had first been told him and believe the Letter false;
and for *Alcander*, that he shou'd go look for the
Olive-leaf, and no doubt he wou'd find it. This
Rallery of the Abbots, tho innocent did nevertheless affect *Philocrates* and *Alcander*, who went
from his Lodgings very melancholy, and much dif-
gusted with what had happen'd to them.

FINIS.

T - #0052 - 270225 - C0 - 186/123/16 [18] - CB - 9780754609872 - Gloss Lamination